My Office Is A 3-Ring Circus!

The Roar Of The Crowd

"Judy walks her walk, talks her talk, and lives her philosophies. Whenever I'm in any type of business crisis or dilemma, I rely on her strategies to straighten things out."
—Tom Budas, best friend and King of the Catch Phrase

"When I first met Judy many years ago, I was amazed that this articulate, classy girl in Beverly Hills was once with the circus. Her voice first captures your attention. The next thing you know, you have been totally enthralled in a conversation that is not only educational but entertaining."
—Kathleen Cover, friend and professional advisor

"My professional and personal relationship with Judy is successful because of the way we roll with the punches. We aren't daunted by change. She does tend to want to be the client in our relationship, but I'm still training her."
—Casey Jones, Caliente tropics Resort, Palm Springs

"Judy is the Dalai Lama of survival through ReInvention."
—Clarke Weigle, former husband

"Judy is the most logic-driven person I know. Even at age five, Judy thought the time spent in Kindergarten could be used more effectively, and quit right after the December gift exchange."
—Lisa Cooper Jensen, friend since age three

"Judy's leadership was developing at age ten, as president of the neighborhood Crispy Critter Club, named after our favorite cereal. We impeached Judy when she got too bossy. The group disbanded because we actually needed her leadership and vision. I think Judy learned a lesson about leadership, too."
—Jeri McFadden, Judy's sister

My Office Is A 3-Ring Circus!

✦

Must I Take Orders From Clowns?

The Ultimate Guide to Building a Bolder, More Balanced & Re-Imaged Career.

JUDITH M. WEIGLE

iUniverse, Inc.
Bloomington

My Office Is A 3-Ring Circus!
Must I Take Orders From Clowns?

iUniverse books may be ordered through booksellers or by contacting:

iUniverse
1663 Liberty Drive
Bloomington, IN 47403
www.iuniverse.com
1-800-Authors (1-800-288-4677)

ISBN: 978-0-5953-5185-5 (sc)
ISBN: 978-0-5957-9882-7 (ebk)

Printed in the United States of America

iUniverse rev. date: 06/15/2011

To My Parents, James & Julia Eppolito

Contents

The Midway: Your Show Is About To Begin

Ironically, many people describe their workplaces by saying, "It's like a three-ring circus in there!" They mean that everything's crazy, there's no focus, no one's in chargex, and the inmates are running the asylum. That's the exact opposite of a *real* circus, which is perhaps the most tightly focused business institution in the world. It has to be. You're talking about moving the equivalent of a small town, complete with a few hundred people, dozens of trucks, wild animals, rigging, and circus tents, so as to put on live and dangerous shows twice daily, March through November, before thousands of people each show.

When people refer to their offices as a three-ring circus they aren't referencing the circus *I* know! *My* circus—the Clyde Beatty-Cole Bros. Circus, the company where I worked for six years, between 1980-1987, as marketing director, contracting agent, elephant ride ticket seller, and Dancing Bear—is not only organized, but is also a laboratory for cutting edge communication skills, providing help with the psychology of working with volatile personalities, both human and animal. To many people, the circus might appear to be the least likely model for outstanding business practices than anyone might imagine. Shockingly, it is the *best* example of an excellent business model, more than any company I have yet to encounter.

And it's fun. After all, it's the circus! Lions, tigers, the Sideshow, beautiful girls in sequins riding the backs of elephants and stallions, acrobats hurtling themselves through space, cotton candy, and a live band that puts everyone in a great mood. The circus, as a classroom, is pure fun.

The purpose of this book is to share with you the business strategies, philosophies, and lessons I learned while working with this wonderful and unbelievably organized group of circus people. I had more fun on the job than anyone is entitled to have. During my four years as marketing director, I coordinated the advertising, publicity, and promotion campaigns in approximately 25 cities a year. I traveled by car three weeks in advance of the towns I was assigned. All tolled, I promoted about 100 cities. One year I worked as contracting agent, traveling six months ahead of the show, establishing the routing schedule throughout the eastern half of the country. Eventually I ended up as a performer for one year. I worked as the Dancing Bear in 1985, the year I married the circus bandleader, Clarke Weigle. That year I traveled *with* the circus, touring to about 120 cities. I think you'll be highly entertained by the problems I was given to solve throughout my circus tenure, and enlightened by the lessons I learned. I bet many of those experiences are quite similar to the ones you face in your work life every day—sans wild animals.

Indeed, our journey starts, not with the animals, the rides, or the clowns . . . our journey starts with a weathered red wooden folding chair. It's nothing special, really, yet the placement of it is compelling, sitting in calm repose next to Jim the Sideshow Barker, on his elevated platform adorning the entrance to the Sideshow tent. You are strategically forced to focus on that red chair as Jim goes through his spiel.

In marketing terms, the Sideshow is an *upsell*. You know you're going to pay an admission to see the two-hour circus show in the Big Top. Now the circus wants to find ways to separate you from a little more cash. Nothing wrong with that. You've come to be entertained and the circus has many unique ways of entertaining you. But what's with that little red chair?

That's exactly the question that Jim wants you to ask. What's that chair *doing* there? Jim circles the chair, points to the chair, and assigns it a tacit force and mission. The chair, throughout Jim's pitch, develops a legend and life of its own. Yet it just sits in the middle of the raised platform stage. As Jim's eloquent pitch grows in fervor, so grows the mystery and power of that little red chair.

There must be something important about it. Otherwise, why would Jim be circling the chair as he speaks, pointing to it, and talking about how "this red chair is only the beginning of what you'll see inside?"

Step back a moment and you'll notice that you're on the Midway of the circus. You are surrounded by a symphony of color and activity. The blue and white striped Big Top, the length of a football field, is directly in front of you. To the right of the Big Top entrance are the food concession trucks serving delectable doses of freshly popped corn, hot dogs, pink and blue cotton candy, and cold, candy-flavored crushed ice cones. Behind you is the elephant ride, with groups of children and parents anxiously waiting their turn to jump on Frieda the Friendly Elephant. The novelty booth, selling souvenir toys, is positioned adjacent to Frieda. To your left, in a neatly formed row, are the moon bounce and the ticket wagon. Everything on the Midway is logistically placed to funnel people into the main entrance of the big tent.

Jim is a sight to see, reminiscent of a Wild West medicine man, outfitted in a striped vest over a rolled cuff, white cotton shirt, and black pants with boots, pacing back and forth above the gathering crowd, talking on the microphone, waving his arms. Sometimes Miss Electra comes out with a baby monkey and sits the creature in the chair. Jim likes when this happens. He gets to do his monkey-on-a-stick joke. The monkey will climb on Jim, or Jim will hold the rambunctious primate while he pitches the show. So what's with the chair?

The little red chair is Jim's secret weapon. He uses it as a symbol of excitement, mystery, and anticipation, all to juice the crowd's sense of intrigue for the mysteries inside. The little red chair has significance equal to our imaginations.

The Barker forces you to start envisioning all the extraordinary sites, inordinately gifted people, and incredible displays of physical ability that you'll see inside the Sideshow tent—all through the hook of the chair.

No matter how fabulous an orator Jim may be, there's got to be something else that catches your attention and fires your mind . . . that little red chair. Then, and only then, are you open to reaching for your wallet and buying the additional admission to the Sideshow.

Jim is circling that chair as he speaks, saying the magic words, "Ladies and Gentlemen, Step right up! What you will see is going to amaze you and confound you, thrill you and delight you, and change you for ever more!"

Who knew that the circus understood human psychology so well? I had no idea, that's for sure. I would never have predicted that my six years with the circus would serve as a vehicle for establishing my business techniques, while presenting me with on-the-job situations that forced me to understand the power I had to control my business decisions.

I learned marketing, publicity, promotion, sales, and negotiating. The demands of working with a traveling circus taught me how to use my own resourcefulness to make things happen. Through the culture of this circus, I realized the importance of work ethic values like responsibility, teamwork, commitment, and independence.

So the premise of this book is to share with you business philosophies, strategies, and lessons I learned about succeeding in our work and developing through our career choices, by exploring a part of the business world that I found to be the most *fun*—the circus. In Ring One: "Performance Tools" I will discuss four concepts that will increase your effectiveness in handling commonly problematic business issues that you encounter daily: from resolving emotional conflicts with office bullies, managing unequally balanced relationships with employers and clients, avoiding crises through preplanning and on-the-spot creative thinking, confidently expressing yourself in business relationships, to successful attempts at negotiating. The key concept here is: *you have more power and control than you realize in your business decisions.* The Performance Tools will be explained through actual situations that happened to me while working for the circus. In "A Pride of Circus Stories" you'll see how these strategies were used to deal with potentially disastrous situations. Who doesn't have crises in their workplaces?

In Ring Two: "Performance Tips" you'll receive concepts and techniques that will be your vehicles for establishing power and control in your daily business life. The key here is: *you can create, choose, and change the way you express power and control in your business relationships.* You will receive effective ways to work from a position of strength and confidence, and develop greater self-respect as a result.

Finally, we'll turn to Ring Three: "Performance Tricks." Most people choose their careers based solely on the work that the job entails. They don't stop to think about the aesthetics that they want to build into their careers. They don't consider, before they embark on those careers, about the lifestyle they want to have, versus the lifestyle that the work would cause them to have. I suggest that choosing the work over the lifestyle is putting the cart before the horse. I'll show you another way to choose your career. Here's the key: *define how you want to live; envision the types of people with whom you want to associate; and, use your favorite skills and talents.*

I didn't grow up with a lifelong passion to join the circus. I'd never even set foot on circus property until my first day of work with the Clyde Beatty-Cole Bros. Circus. My career with the circus was the epitome of the lifestyle goal I set for myself in college: to travel and work in as many different places in the world as possible; and to work with as many different cultures of people, too. With those goals in mind, I was drawn to the classified ad for Circus Marketing Directors in my hometown newspaper, the *Pittsburgh Press*. That ad was my little red chair. That ad was my ticket towards fulfilling my *workstyle* goals, lifestyle combined with work, while using all the skills and talents I explored in college.

After graduating from Duquesne University in 1975, I worked at a variety of companies before I read that life-changing classified ad in April of 1980. It was only a matter of time before the right job would come along that would give me the lifestyle I desired, and satisfy my vision of a fulfilling career choice.

Also in Ring Three I'll show you just how to put a game plan together so that you can deal with inevitable change that occurs in every industry, and mitigate the fear that change can bring. You can learn to work in anticipation of the rewards you'll receive in the business life you choose if you are open to change, resistant of fear, and agree to an individualistic way of thinking.

The book concludes with some reflective thoughts from poignant observers in Backstage: "The Critics Speak."

And it all begins . . . with that little red chair!

Without further ado, come right in! Step right up! You're in for the show of your life!

Ring One: Performance Tools

I want to share with you the Performance Tools of Mental Chess, Creative Logic, Crisis Avoidance, and Idea Energy. The Performance Tools can magically transform out-of-control events into sanity-driven experiences. They are your resources for outthinking any power suckers around you, and for maintaining control over your decisions and reactions to power-draining problems. We all need strategies to maintain power and control in our work, and ultimately our careers. The philosophy of the Performance Tools is this: *you have more power and control than you realize in your business decisions.*

The basic idea behind the Performance Tools is that they give you the ability to exercise more power and control over your responses to unwieldy circumstances that your work environment can create. They are effective mental exercises to use with your employers, your co-workers, and your clients. These exercises and thought processes will give you the ability to change the course of crazy-making events, to settle disagreements, and to reestablish ground rules. The Performance Tools can help you build a strong foundation, or in circus terms, secure rigging, for professional growth.

Let's distinguish between power and control. Power is the ability to act, to make things happen. Control is the exercise of power. Power is not given to us by anyone; it exists within each one of us. We must take hold of our power and use it. In a balanced relationship of mutual respect, neither party has total control or total power over the other. If you're an employer or a client, you'll never get full value out of your employees or vendor/consultants if you rigidly try to control them. For the employees and vendor/consultants reading this book, I want to show you how to use your power so that you don't fear your employers and clients.

1

Exercising power allows you to control and win more emotional showdowns. People accept powerlessness in business relationships by not understanding a core principle of winning: in order to win, you must act like you have nothing to lose. This is a high wire strategy that will position you above the crowded field of employees and vendor/consultants. Acting like you have nothing to lose positions you to speak your mind, establish your boundaries, and hold firm to your convictions.

We all need help responding to emotional showdowns. You know those drama scenes all too well: you're being manipulated, you're being bullied, you're being challenged, you're being asked to compromise the way you think, or you're being disrespected. Whatever the case, you now have an arsenal of protection in the Performance Tools to combat fierce aggressors—your fellow workers, employers, and clients.

Mental Chess

Mental Chess is a thought process and a communication skill. Mental Chess is engaged when two or more people with different points of view, and slightly different goals, reach an impasse of agreement. Each of the parties has individual goals that they wish to achieve. I contend that the healthiest way to reach those individual goals is to establish a collective goal. In order to establish a collective goal, conversation has to take place that allows each person to communicate his or her needs. When the communication of our needs takes place in an open, honest, and respectful way, a balanced solution has the best chance of serving each party equitably.

When both sides feel like they've won, the relationship moves forward in a positive way. In a normal chess game only one person can win. I've tried to change the rules of chess a bit with the idea of Mental Chess creating two winners. From my philosophical point of view, Mental Chess can help you manipulate a relationship imbalance so that the relationship is the winner.

Let's assign names to the players of our Mental Chess game. Employees and vendor/consultants, are known as "sellers." Employers and clients are "buyers." Buyers and sellers have different roles and different responsibilities. Yet, buyers and sellers are working towards the same goal—making money, conducting business. Mental Chess games decide power matches between buyers and sellers when disagreements occur. We have to know how to play the game correctly so we don't get creamed.

In order to win, act like you have nothing to lose. Sellers risk loss any time they negotiate with buyers. A seller who fails to make a convincing argument may risk the loss of income, the loss of a promotion, the loss of privileges, or the loss of a job. Don't fear loss, because loss, through a well-orchestrated strategy and an ethically supported position, is not a loss at all. The seller gains in strength of character and strength of will by just playing Mental Chess, engaging in open dialogue. With strength of character and will, you'll win the most important part of the chess match—freedom of expression. With mastery of self-expression you will be a stronger contender in future power matches. If played from the heart, you generally won't lose. You may compromise a bit, but you typically won't lose.

There's no more important time to use Mental Chess skills than when the seller is faced with a losing proposition. In business communication, just as on the chessboard, we have multiple choices for our responses, our strategies and our positions. *First*, have the courage of your convictions to fight for what you think is right. You have to communicate your needs and the logic that supports those needs. *Second*, consider the consequences that follow any move, but not so much that it causes inaction. *Third*, make the move that supports the best outcome for you and the relationship. You are constantly engaged in power matches whether you know it or not. You may as well be a contender by knowing how to play the game.

When I was growing up, I always loved playing chess. When I entered the business world, I realized that negotiations were very much like chess moves. You don't have to be a chess grand master to know that success in chess comes from considering the board, thinking through all your options, and then choosing the move you evaluate to be the best. The same thing is true in the business world. You've got to think things through before you make a move. Sometimes you only have a minute to think and respond. You've got to ask yourself both what's important to you, and fair for the other side, too. You have to ask yourself what you are willing to risk—your time, perhaps your money, or your reputation—as you are lobbying for what you want.

We are happiest when we are in control. Conversely, we're fearful in combative situations where people and events threaten our control. Remember, you can *always* control your reactions; and you can *always* control your behavior. Mental Chess comes down to the idea that you can maintain some degree of control, and therefore power, if you accept the idea that you always have options, and look for those options instead of opting out of the game.

It's important to remember that even the best chess players don't win every time! Not all of the risks that you run will pay off. Sometimes you will pay a price, but hopefully just a short-term price. The main thing is to be in the game, to be studying the board, and to act boldly and decisively, once you have figured out what is best for you, and what you consider to be fair for your friendly opponent.

Mental Chess requires us to remember that we do have the power, and the right, to speak our minds. We have the responsibility to express our positions if we want to advance. If we don't stand up for ourselves, if we don't explain what we want and why we deserve it, we won't get it.

It is essential to know what your values are and to stay committed to those values and goals. If you have clearly defined values and goals you generally get much more out of negotiable situations than if you don't. Know exactly what you want, and know what you are willing to walk away from. Mental Chess, in its purest form, can direct you to walk away from a deal that does not comport with your values, your self-image, or your sense of right and wrong.

Creative Logic

You're on the spot. Someone is expecting something from you that is unforeseen, unfair, or inappropriate. Your power and control are on the line. What do you do?

If you're like a lot of people, the answer is . . . absolutely nothing! Many of us freeze and go into fear mode when confronted with spontaneous and challenging situations. Then we act like ostriches by burying our heads in the sand and hoping the whole thing will somehow go away. The only problem with burying your head in the sand is that another part of your anatomy is perilously exposed! Need I say more?

Creative Logic can help you craft a practical response to an immediate and volatile issue by *first*, remaining calm; *second*, dissecting the circumstances; *third*, considering your options; and *fourth*, formulating a strategy and making a bold decision. Not easy, but doable if you're willing to take a chance with decision-making. If you can put fear aside and take a stand that isn't as moderate or as safe as you're used to, you can take back control. The reason we need a Performance Tool like Creative Logic is because we are generally less than secure and practical in stressful situations. The human mind works more on emotion than logic. That's why it's necessary to strip away emotion when we are being challenged. Train yourself to remain calm so that you don't buckle under pressure.

Having a sense of humor is helpful, too. The circus stories I am about to tell you have a degree of humor in them. But so do your work stories. Who's the clown in your office? Who's the ringmaster? Who's the magician who practices slight-of-hand? Who makes the roar of the lion? Here's an exercise for you: replay how you would have handled yourself in a previous contentious situation using Creative Logic to influence the outcome. Pull the event apart and figure out the variety of responses you could have used to create the outcome that would have suited you and the event better. Then try to blueprint that approach for the next emotional showdown. Could you have used humor to affect the outcome? Humor does have a way of taking the edge and the absurdity out of a volatile event.

The toughest part of Creative Logic is acting without emotion, and with a sense of humor. It's so hard to use common sense, to be able to see logic, when tempers are flaring and people are crusading for their own causes. But someone's got to do it. Why not you? Why not practice being the voice of reason? Making unexpected yet calculated decisions with a dash of humor will reinforce your position of control. Bold strokes for bold folks.

Crisis Avoidance

A problem most business people face is that their short-term goal is noon and their long-term goal is midnight. The reality is that congress has yet to repeal Murphy's Law but most people persist in making the fatal assumption that "everything is going to be all right." They only rely on plan A. I contend that having a plan B always at the ready is intrinsic to maintaining control over your work.

In order to maintain control in your work, you always have to prepare for the worst that could happen and set yourself up with alternate solutions for any imaginable catastrophe. Stuff just happens! On the positive side of Crisis Avoidance, get in the habit of challenging yourself beyond your job description by knowing more than you are required to know; you'll be prepared for any change of events that might occur at any moment.

We'll review humorous circus stories in the next few pages and examine critical events that were saved by crisis planning and quick thinking. Even on the most simplistic level, crises can be avoided by forethought and planning. In my most current involvement within the entertainment industry, producing music and dance shows for corporate events, I found that performers could show up forgetting everything from batteries, to music stands and costumes. I always made it my business to bring along extra staff and extra supplies to every party for the simple reason that I could never predict what might go wrong. My philosophy is that I'm not being paid for my good intentions; I'm being paid for my ability to predict and avoid crises. Most crises can be avoided with advance planning.

In your line of work, think through all the things that could go wrong and affect the positive outcome of the projects you're working on. Make a plan B for each possible crisis, no matter how far-fetched. Act on the advice you receive from those who have been before you. Chances are there is someone in your firm who can give you sage counsel about how to avoid potential and typical crises. We can learn from the solutions of other people.

If your job takes you to out-of-office work sites, come prepared with more support staff, supplies, documentation, and tools of your trade than it is your habit to bring. If you are in charge of hiring support staff for a project, hire more people than you think you'll need. What if you're a caterer and a dozen more guests show up to an event than planned? You'll need more staff. Always have the complete file of the project with you. With all the paperwork in hand, including the original contract and any changes thereto, you will have a much easier time maintaining control over your work, your reputation, and your future revenue, as you will have control through information flow. Keep plenty of supplies in the trunk of your car. Remember: supplies beat surprise! That's what this Performance Tool is all about.

Idea Energy

Idea Energy is a term that was given to me by a dear friend, Karrie O'Brien, whom I met through a client in Palm Springs, CA many years after the circus. One day over lunch I was helping Karrie to brainstorm ideas for a new business venture she wanted to explore. In the midst of my extemporaneous musings about positioning and framing Karrie's unique skills and talents, she stopped me and said, "Judy, you have Idea Energy!" Perfect phrase.

What Idea Energy means to me, in its broadest sense, is a self-generating force that motivates us to look inside of ourselves to see who we are, to ascertain what we want out of life through our work, and then to create a career for ourselves that is uniquely us. We all have skills that can either be mainstreamed, or positioned to serve us in unusual ways. Our lives should be about following our gut instincts, being true to our natures, and setting lifestyle goals. If you're in your right environment, and functioning productively, the money will come.

Perfect career choices are always available, but how could we possibly know what we want to do until we know who we want to be and how we want to live? The state of the economy, the state of technology, our unique skills and talents, and our individual lifestyle requirements can combine so that we can make the best choices and actually enjoy our work lives instead of suffering through them as so many people do.

The Performance Tool of Idea Energy fuels your ability to deal with fear of change in your career. A bad economy and advanced technology are two of the biggest culprits that effect major change in your employment status, quite often before you're ready to change. If life has forced change upon you, move with it! This refers to the job you have currently and the industry in which you work. You don't have to fear change. You can use change as a positive motivator.

Consider this: the wealthiest people in the world are responsible for change. Check out the *Fortune 500* Wealthiest People in America list. Who has been at the top of the list for quite some time? Bill Gates. Is not Mr. Gates responsible for creating change in technology that created change in our workplaces, and subsequently in our careers and in the shelf life of our jobs?? Read further down the list and you will see many people who are responsible for change through business innovation and technological advancement. Change, if used as a springboard for innovation, can bring us wealth and happiness. The barons of wealth are the barons of change.

Personal growth is the other factor that creates the need for change in our careers. It generally takes an extremely traumatic event to get us to stop and reassess our lives. Are we doing what we want with our skills and talents? Are we living the life that makes the most sense for us? Or are we running plays out of someone else's play book? I ask this question: Why should it take a crisis to provoke the kind of internal discussion about our career paths that each of us should be having all the time?

If where you are professionally and financially isn't right for you, change. The energy of new ideas can be the driving force behind finding the perfect work for you. Create some new usage for your special skills, talents, and ideas.

We all know the expression that the devil we know is preferable to the devil we don't know. Another way of saying this is that most people are motivated more by the fear of loss than by the desire for gain. In other words, we hate change. We fear it, and we do everything we can to avoid it. The fact is that change is beneficial to us. We naturally tend to think that change means a change for the worst. In reality, change can be a great way to move to a much more fulfilling place.

Recognize that you will always have to deal with change if you want to grow in your career. As new technology and the economy encroach on your business, change with it by reevaluating your industry and your role within it. Think about where your industry might be in two to five years and change the role you play now to keep relevant and grow.

You have many skills and talents that are marketable. It's all a matter of how you position and frame those skills and talents, and how you create a demand for them, that determines your level of Idea Energy.

A PRIDE OF CIRCUS STORIES

Clowning Around With Crisis

Panama City, Florida. A bad town for clowns.

Especially for combative clowns who didn't like each other. Clowns who didn't respect each other. Clowns who had a bad history together. I, in all my innocence, was about to learn a lesson about clowns and crisis.

Before I joined the circus, two of the best clowns in Clown Alley, Bubbles and Bonkers, had developed a very bad relationship. When they fought, it was no laughing matter. It's not that different from any two coworkers in any workplace who can't stand one another—the whole department suffers. Or if the disagreement is at a high enough level, the whole company pays the price. When coworkers hate each other, the results are never pretty. Of course, here you had two clowns who were supposed to be entertaining thousands of people at each show. Instead they fostered a rivalry with a bitterness that became legendary within the circus community.

Their fights were grand, and it became clear to everyone at the circus that one or both soon would have to go. Bonkers the Clown ended up leaving the circus, and under his real name, became the marketing director of a shopping mall in Panama City, Florida. Bubbles the Clown remained with the circus in the role of advance clown. Advance clowns travel by themselves in their own trailers and meet up with marketing directors/promoters, people like myself, two or three days before the circus comes to town. The role of the advance clown is to create awareness of the circus, fulfill scheduled media interviews, and entertain through prearranged promotional events.

For the first time since their battles under our big tent, Bubbles and Bonkers were about to cross paths, and red clown noses again. Things never turn out well when you're dealing with combative clowns.

I was tipped off about the feud by the circus office when I received my briefing on Panama City. The extent of this historical quarrel was about to unfold when I picked up Bubbles, camped outside the mall. It was five in the morning on that fateful day. We had a 5:30 a.m. live TV appearance. Bubbles was in full clown makeup and costume when I gave him his itinerary, driving down to the TV station. That morning, the itinerary explained, he and Bonkers, who had never lost his love of clowning despite his new career at the mall, would put on a Junior Clown Academy makeup class and magic show for area children. The local TV station and the Panama City Mall sponsored the Junior Clown Academy. Kids wrote in to explain why, in fifty words or less, they wanted to attend. The itinerary explained that Bubbles would conduct the Junior Clown Academy, while Bonkers would join Bubbles in a magic show following the makeup class.

Since I had come on the scene long after Bonkers had departed the circus, I had no idea how he felt about the combative clown history between the two men. Bubbles certainly remembered.

"By the way," I said, as we rolled down the highway to the TV station, "you'll be performing with Bonkers, now the mall's marketing director." I was about to set off the clown equivalent of World War III.

"Bonkers?" Bubbles asked with concern in his voice. "Don't you understand the problems we've had together?"

I nodded, waiting for the storm to break. "I have *some* information about you and Bonkers. He was before my time, but I'm sure you've moved past this by now, right?"

Bubbles, arms crossed, replied, "No, I won't perform with Bonkers, nor will I make the magic show part of my promotional pitch."

Maybe it was early. Neither of us had had *enough* coffee yet. I thought I'd misunderstood what I'd heard.

"Did you say, 'No, I won't'?" I asked.

Bubbles nodded. "I won't appear with him. Period. End of story."

"You have to," I replied calmly.

"No, I don't," Bubbles said.

What??? This was insanity. I was driving down the highway in Panama City, Florida, at ten minutes after five in the morning, with a recalcitrant clown. "It's not up to you," I said, getting a little agitated. "This is your job. The mall is hosting our visit. The promotion *has* to take place. You've got to do it." Bubbles just shook his head. His clown makeup exaggerated the effect of his pouting. I was driving with a pouting, recalcitrant clown.

"You've got to do it," I said, now more than a bit peeved. "Have you completely lost your mind? It's not our decision to change advance promotions! This is our job!"

"I hate Bonkers," Bubbles said obstinately, staring me down. "There's no way I'm going to perform with him. You just don't understand our history." A moment passed when Bubbles added, "You can't make me!"

Suddenly I pulled the car over to the side of the road, brakes screeching.

"Get out!" I ordered.

Bubbles, shocked, looked at me.

"Get out of the car!" I said angrily. "If you're not going to do what you're supposed to do, then get out of my car. And take your toys with you!"

"But—but—but . . ." Bubbles stammered.

"If you're not going to appear with Bonkers, then get the hell out of my car! Right now!"

Bubbles was shocked at the severity of my tone and by the resoluteness of my decision. There was no turning back for me. I had made up my mind. Bubbles had to go in order for me to keep control. He could see I meant business.

Bubbles got out of the car. I drove away.

Dawn was breaking in Panama City as I looked back and saw a fully dressed clown, holding his cardboard box of clown toys, standing at the side of the road, possibly the most unusual site I have ever seen in my rearview mirror. All of a sudden I realized the enormity of what I had done. Bubbles was supposed to be at the station in just ten minutes to make people laugh, do charming tricks, and promote a series of events to boost advance ticket sales. And I had thrown him out of my car. Was I insane? Would they fire me for this? Or was it the only intelligent thing to do?

The only reason I felt comfortable taking such a drastic stand with Bubbles was because I had a plan B upon which to rely. On a much earlier trip, Bubbles had once said to me, "If I ever keel over dead, and you have media interviews that must be fulfilled, just put on a red nose. You'll get attention and laughter, and you'll be able to handle any interview. A clown wearing a red nose is funny enough, but a businessperson dressed in a suit and wearing a red nose is absolutely hilarious. You're bound to get laughs no matter what you say."

I know good advice when I hear it, so I went out that very day and bought a bunch of ping-pong balls, cut them in half, and painted them with red nail polish. I had half a dozen of these trick noses in my glove compartment, for just such emergencies like now. It was time to go to plan B, Operation Red Nose.

I drove to the TV station with my red nose strategically placed on my face, the half ping-pong ball covered in red nail polish. "I'm with the circus," I explained, and everybody laughed and smiled. I told them that our clown was unavoidably detained. I didn't elaborate as to the reasons why. I explained that I knew everything that was in his act, and I would be happy to do the TV spot for him.

The interview went on, and everything was fine. That red nose saved the day. It really is true. If anyone, especially a regular person in a business suit, wears a red nose, everyone is going to laugh. I was able to do a competent job of filling in for Bubbles, accomplish the goals established for the interview, and thus the circus itself. So all was well, at least in television land. But what about my job?

As soon as I left the station, I called the home office in Deland, Florida, to explain what had happened. They already knew. It turned out that Bubbles had been promptly picked up by the local Panama City Police for walking alongside a highway in a full disguise. Apparently, in Florida, and perhaps other states as well, it is against the law to be walking along the side of a highway in a disguise of costume and full makeup. The police need to be able to identify individuals at all times.

Bubbles the Clown had been unavoidably detained in Panama City. The police brought him to the mall, and right into the marketing director's office, that of Bonkers the former Clown. Bubbles had to explain what happened, and isn't it ironic that he had to explain it to Bonkers? Bubbles, Bonkers, and the police called the home office to explain their side of the story while I was out.

Did I lose my job over this? No. The home office was well aware that Bubbles, on occasion, had been giving all the marketing directors fits for years. He could be high-strung, high maintenance, and sometimes hard to work with. Granted, it does take something of an artistic temperament to be a good clown, but Bubbles constantly pushed the limits of his art.

As far as the home office was concerned, they were delighted that somebody had finally taught Bubbles a lesson. Who knew that a glove compartment full of red noses could save the day?

Performance Tools:
Crisis Avoidance, Creative Logic

Crisis Avoidance was the name of the game and the Performance Tool that saved the day for me in Panama City, Florida. When Bubbles sullenly announced that he would not take the stage with his old rival, Bonkers, a crisis was on my hands. What were my options? Could I have told Bonkers, the marketing director of the mall, that he wasn't going to get to perform as a clown in the magic show, which was the mall's promotional event? Was I going to acquiesce to the antics of my somewhat high-strung colleague? No, and no. These were simply not options, as far as I was concerned. The best way to avoid a crisis was to isolate the cause of the crisis, and thus not allow his petulance to affect in a negative way anyone else involved in the situation—the TV station, Bonkers the Clown, or our relationship with the Panama City Mall. I isolated the cause and then moved past it.

It certainly helped that I had a plan B at hand in the form of those red noses. I found many times after that experience that when you put a red nose on your face, you are instantly funny, and instantly accepted wherever you go as an ambassador of the circus. Red noses were my plan B, my Crisis Avoidance. When crises come up in your workplace, do you have plan Bs at hand? This is the time to start thinking through what your plan Bs might look like. A red nose may not work for you, so it may have to be something else. But the concept is the same; you've got to have backup plans. What are yours?

The Performance Tool of Creative Logic also played a role in this story. When Bubbles was pitching his fit in my car, I had two choices: give in, or stand my ground. If I had given in, I would have redefined the terms of my relationship with Bubbles . . . forever. Not only that, but word of the incident would almost certainly have filtered back to the home office, and it would have been understood that Judy could be pushed around. This is exactly the wrong reputation to have. It is essential to know how to take control back in a tense situation. Being fluent in Creative Logic will generate respect for you, and confidence in your management skills from your employers and clients. I'm not talking about going ballistic at every perceived slight. I am talking about recognizing when your authority and control are on the line. It is simply not optional at those times to do anything other than stand your ground, maintain control and self-respect, along with the respect of those around you. Bubbles might not have had to like me, but he certainly had to respect me, as we were both employees of the same company.

When my logic detector pointed to the red zone, I knew that I had to act, and act with power. That's why I threw Bubbles out of the car; and I would urge anyone in a similar position to take the same kind of drastic action. Of course, I didn't simply open the door and shove him out of a moving vehicle. I did stop on the shoulder of the road. And I gave him a choice: he could either stay, and accept the responsibilities of his job, as uncomfortable as it might have been for him—another performance with his old enemy, Bonkers the Clown; or he could walk, literally. Logical, eh?

Hey, I don't put up with clowns or their catastrophes! Neither should you.

Don't Take Orders From Clowns

It was October, and once again Bubbles the Clown and I were working together, doing advance work for the circus in the town of Muscle Shoals, Alabama. Our job was to create awareness for the circus in a proven, enjoyable, and traditional way. We would put on a Junior Clown Academy makeup class at a local shopping mall. Bubbles would do magic for all the children and their parents to see as they were passing through the mall. A select group of children, who had already won their admission through a newspaper contest, would be able to experience a session of clown makeup lessons with Bubbles. Bubbles had forgiven me for my role in his brush with the law in Florida. While we might not have been the best of friends, we were certainly able to work together toward the goal of promoting the circus. A little clown magic, a little clown makeup at a shopping mall . . . what could go wrong?

With Bubbles, just about anything.

Sales were brisk and I was pleased with the school shows and media interviews that Bubbles and I had done so far in Muscle Shoals. I was working out of the circus's temporary ticket booth in the center court area of the mall while Bubbles did his show, which was, as usual, a great success with the children and their parents. For all his temperamental issues, Bubbles had a great way with the kids; there was no denying that. He was truly an excellent clown.

Bubbles finished his show and it was time for the two of us to grab dinner so that we could get ready for another day of clown promotions. Our work was done beautifully. Muscle Shoals was abuzz with news of the circus, and it had looked like we would have two sold out show days. I was packing up the advance sale tickets and money while Bubbles presumably went back to his trailer to change clothes. Bubbles traveled in a small camper attached to a truck. When the circus was contracted to perform at shopping malls, management would let Bubbles hook up to water and electricity on mall property.

I wasn't a witness to the next part of the story. Unfortunately for Bubbles, the individual who filled me in on what happened outside the mall on the way to Bubbles' trailer was a member of the Muscle Shoals Police Force. Yes,

Bubbles got into legal trouble once again. Apparently, after he left the mall to head back to his trailer in the parking lot, Bubbles was accosted by a small group of excited children who thought it was terrific to have a little time alone with a real, live clown. The problem that clowns face universally is that small children simply don't get that there is a human being inside the clown suit; they're not supposed to. They assume that a clown is the same sort of supernatural figure they might encounter in a video game or on TV. So it is not uncommon for children to punch a clown, kick a clown, or even bite a clown. For clowns, these are common occupational hazards.

It can actually get a little frightening for a clown, because if enough small to medium sized children are beating on him, he really has no recourse. A clown isn't supposed to get in a fight with children. That's kind of a code of ethics among clowns. Well, a few kids came up to Bubbles. They began to taunt him, to kick him, and to pull on his costume. Bubbles, according to his testimony to the authorities, repeatedly asked the children to stop, but they would not.

By now, Bubbles and the kids were really mixing it up. The kids had seen the Junior Clown Academy and therefore had an emotional connection to Bubbles. But they had been left in their car by their father, who needed to duck into the mall for a last minute purchase. When the father emerged with purchases in hand, he discovered, to his horror, that a clown in full makeup and costume was attacking his children with a large foam hammer (only one ounce in weight), and kicking at them with his big, floppy cardboard shoes, neither weapon in any way hurtful to the children.

The father, of course, flipped out when he saw this little scene. His kids were having fun battling Bubbles, but the father didn't expect to see a clown in combat with his kids. Bubbles, on the other hand, was hugely aggravated, because there were enough kids to cause him some degree of bodily harm. This is not what a clown bargains for when he sets out on a career of entertaining the young.

The father immediately called the police and explained that a clown had attacked his kids. He wanted the clown arrested for assault and battery. Bubbles, extremely agitated by now, told the gendarmes that he was hitting the children with his large foam hammer and kicking them with his long, floppy cardboard shoes strictly in self-defense, with no physical repercussions. He really feared these kids were going to pull his costume off and discover that a human was inside.

By now, I was on the scene, and found myself in the middle of this extraordinary showdown between an angry clown, an irate father, and a policeman, who was probably trying to keep a straight face throughout the whole calamity. The father had witnessed what he considered a crime, and therefore insisted on pressing charges. The police officer really didn't want to arrest Bubbles, and asked the father if an apology in front of the kids would smooth the whole mess out. If Bubbles had kept his cool, possibly ducked back into the mall and used me for assistance, I would have shielded our august friend and prevented the attack on the children with his foam hammer and floppy shoes. That was Bubbles' first mistake.

Then Bubbles made his second mistake. Bubbles' pride and emotion got in the way and he refused to apologize. Instead, he ordered me, he didn't ask or whisper or suggest, but instead ordered me to use circus ticket money as the bond money that the police officer required in order to prevent Bubbles from spending a night in jail. The deal was that with an apology we would walk away clean; without an apology we had to appear in front of the judge the next morning. Bail money would make the difference between Bubbles staying in jail overnight, or in his trailer.

I don't get ordered around by clowns. And neither should you!

Certainly, my pride was on the line, because you can't go around letting the people who work for you push you around, especially in front of total strangers. Had Bubbles addressed me in any other way, I'm sure I would have been happy to help him try to straighten out this unfortunate catastrophe. After all, I certainly sympathized with his plight. A clown alone is a natural target for abuse. Bubbles could have taken me aside and said quietly, "I don't want to go to jail, Judy. I flipped out. I overreacted. Anybody would have freaked with all those kids taunting and harassing. Could I please ask you to just take care of the situation? I promise it'll never happen again."

I'm not talking about groveling. I'm not talking about abject begging. I'm just talking about the simple respect that one individual owes his or her colleague in the work place. Granted, the parking lot of a mall is not the most usual of work places. The fact is that Bubbles and I did have a common employer, and we were expected to uphold the dignity of our employer. Under stress, Bubbles had snapped, but that did not give him any right to snap at me. Frankly, I was in no mood to help him, now that he was trying to posture in front of the police and the angry dad, not to mention the kids.

Bubbles, a little bit too stubborn for his own good, would not apologize to anyone. After all, as he heatedly pointed out, the kids had started it. Anyone in his position, carrying a large foam hammer and wearing floppy shoes would have used those tools as self-defense. No apology was forthcoming from the clown. Bubbles was rapidly losing what few allies he had. The father was still against him. The cop was turning against him. And by attempting to order me around, I was certainly in no mood to take Bubbles' side. The police officer asked me how I wanted to handle this, since Bubbles was clearly not going to be part of any tidy solution.

"I'm leaning toward putting you in jail," I told a shocked Bubbles. The look in his eyes suggested that I was betraying not just him, but the honor of every clown who had ever put on makeup, juggled, or pushed the life of a spotlight with a broom. I was letting down the whole clown universe.

I didn't care. If Bubbles wanted to flip out, that was his business. If he wanted to do it on company time, in costume, while representing the circus, in front of children, then that was another matter altogether. I told the police that if he wouldn't apologize, they were free, as far as I was concerned, to take him to jail.

The police asked Bubbles one more time if he would care to apologize. Bubbles stood his ground. No apologies.

"In that case," the policeman told the stubborn clown, "You're coming with me."

Bubbles was allowed to return to his trailer, wash off his clown make-up, and put on street clothes before the police led him away. I kept Bubbles' small dog, Kitty (yes, Bubbles had a dog named Kitty), and Bubbles the Clown went off to spend the night in jail.

We're not talking Alcatraz, or Sing Sing—some nightmarish penitentiary. This was actually more like *Andy of Mayberry*. Muscle Shoals is not a big city; they didn't have a lot of crime. For all I know, Bubbles was their first clown ever to face prosecution.

To Bubbles' surprise, the jail cell was actually a lot better than the trailer in which he and Kitty traveled. Bubbles, in fact, enjoyed the honor of being the very first prisoner in a brand new jail cell the town just constructed. Bubbles' last words to me, as he entered his cell, were these: "I bet the home office won't like this." (You could almost hear organ chords in the background!)

The cops, of course, were hysterical. They thought it was incredibly funny to incarcerate a clown. They assured me that nothing bad would happen to him, that he would be able to order takeout from one of the local restaurants, and that he would be completely safe and comfortable during his night behind bars.

I think he had TV, too. The cops and I agreed that maybe Bubbles would learn something from his night in the pen.

The next morning, prior to our court appearance, I had to call the home office, and report the news that I had allowed our advance clown to be taken into custody. Once again, I made "the call" with a certain amount of concern for the future of my own job. I feared that they would have expected me to stand up for Bubbles and make sure that he stayed out of jail, no matter what the price, either in bail money or in damage to my professional standing. After the laughter died down, my supervisor, I'm glad to report, agreed with me about the way I had handled the situation. They understood that once Bubbles acted out of ego, I couldn't be his ally.

That morning, Bubbles awoke to a jailhouse breakfast of biscuits and gravy. (This is Alabama, of course.) He was brought before a magistrate, who ordered him to create no more unscripted clown's play with soft or hard weapons. Bubbles agreed; the case was dismissed; and we resumed our scheduled work of school shows and media interviews.

Was Bubbles a great clown? Absolutely. From a craft standpoint, I worked with none who were better than he. But how well you do your job is only a part of the total picture. You've got to be a team player. You've got to respect the other people with whom you work. And you can't treat people you work with as if they are subordinates, especially when there's an audience present and watching.

Performance Tool: Creative Logic

First, my logic alarm sounded big time when, in the parking lot outside of the Muscle Shoals Mall in Alabama, Bubbles ordered me in front of the assembled tableau of uniformed officer, irate father, children, and assorted bystanders to clean up his mess. Even though the foam hammer and cardboard shoes could never have hurt anyone, it was still unacceptable behavior for a circus clown to pummel children. We all know when we are being pushed around, and it's not acceptable to take it. After all, if we do allow that sort of behavior once, we are essentially giving that person the green light to act that same way whenever he or she so chooses. Responding to disrespectful orders must be taboo in our business world. We have to stand up to corporate bullies just as we had to stand up to schoolyard bullies when we were kids. We cannot let people roll over us. Our logic detector demands no less.

Second, my logic processing kicked in. I thought it was time for Bubbles to learn a lesson in priorities and appropriate behavior. The only way he could learn these lessons would be for me to get in Creative Logic mode and take a course of action to help him recognize that his thinking was way off the beam. My choices were clear: accept Bubbles' unacceptable behavior or let him go to jail. In the practice of Creative Logic I calmly defined the problem, weighed my options, and went in for the kill. The clown needed help. The father needed action. The police needed a decision, and I needed a hot meal and control back. I went for a two part plan: get Bubbles to the police station and hopefully shock him into common sense with an apology; or, at least check out the jail and make sure it was clean and comfortable for a quick overnight visit. When I saw that the jail had better accommodations than Bubbles' trailer, coupled with his unchanged attitude, I chose to let him stay the night.

Did Bubbles learn a lesson? I'm sure he did, although some people have to be hit in the head with a foam hammer a few times before they start listening to reason. Even though my dignity was as much at risk as Bubbles', I remained calm. I was able to examine my choices, to get him off the hook or let him face the consequences of his actions, then make what was for me the right choice. That's Creative Logic in action: remain calm, understand the circumstances, consider your choices, and make a bold decision. The playful side of me knew that this incident would make great fodder for stories in the future.

The people you work with don't always have to like you. But they absolutely have to respect you. Your behavior has to breed respect. I think that's the clear lesson that Bubbles took away from his night in jail in Muscle Shoals.

I don't take orders from clowns; nobody should!

Feed Your Friends to the Lions

As I frequently tell my clients, "If you like everyone in your workplace, you're truly a special person." Nobody likes everybody. It's just not possible. It's just not human. And in the workplace, it's just not likely.

Quite frankly, there are a lot of people in most organizations who would try the patience of a saint. How do they hang on to their jobs? Maybe they've got pictures of the C.E.O. in a compromising position with . . . never mind. Regardless of how the unlikable in your workplace got there, be they coworkers, supervisors, underlings, clients or customers, the fact is that sometimes we just wish we could do something malicious, calculating, or compromising with them.

The circus is no different. When groups of people are living, working, and traveling together in close quarters, under cramped circumstances, day after day, and often year after year, they have an all too human tendency, on occasion, to despise one another.

I wish I could say I was immune from such petty qualms and dislikes, but the fact is that I am just as human as anyone else. There was one particular individual, Manny, who could make me crazy at the slightest provocation. There was just something highly annoying and upsetting about Manny. I'm sure you could fill in the blank with someone in your office. That's just life.

One evening, about half an hour before show time, Manny happened to walk a little too close to the lion cage. Apparently, the lion shared the same low opinion of him that I had. Imagine that! The lion, whom most of us thought of as a sweet, if large, Tabby, suddenly roused from his usual torpor and with a mighty roar, took a swipe at Manny, his paw extending through the bars of his cage and missing our mutual enemy by a hairsbreadth.

The target of the lion's wrath, naturally enough, was terrified, and ran from the beast in a most unmasculine manner. Up until that moment, Manny was about as super macho as anyone in the circus. I wasn't the only one who witnessed the drive-by swiping. In fact, just about everyone in the opening number of the circus saw it happen, because they were lining up to get ready to start the evening's performance.

Needless to say, a good time was had by all.

It was about this time that I had begun to search for a new way of marketing the circus on the radio. Like most creative people, I get tired of doing the same thing over and over, even if that thing is successful. The freshest ideas can seem stale, especially after trundling them into radio stations for years on end. I felt a sense of burnout with some of the marketing promotions that I had been using, and was on the lookout for something new.

Then came that incident with the drive-by swiping.

Coupled with this, I noticed that every time I introduced myself to anybody in any town, the immediate and overwhelming response was, "Oh, my office is like a three-ring circus every day!" I realized that this constant response represented a common denominator with the general public. And that's how this radio promotion, *Feed Your Friends to the Lions*, was born. After all, what's on people's minds when they drive to and from work? That's right, work. And what do most people do when they're thinking about the office? They frequently run through situations and people who make them feel powerless. So I wanted to create a promotion that would call upon this connection to the circus that most people had—the comparison of their office to the circus—along with tapping into the sense of control all people need. I wanted to give them a way to vent frustrations without endangering themselves with their companies.

The more people to whom I told the story about the lion who nearly killed our Work Jerk (every office has a Work Jerk!), the more great reactions I got. Everybody thought it was the funniest thing in the world because the individual only got scared and didn't actually get hurt. That's when it hit me. I would develop a new promotional vehicle for radio that would invite listeners to call into the station and describe someone in their lives that they wished they could feed to the lions. I figured it would be a great tension-reliever.

The results were sensational. Switchboards exploded at every radio station where I brought the idea. It seemed as though just about everybody had someone who deserved to be fed to the king of beasts.

Actually, I noticed an intriguing, if somewhat disturbing pattern. Pretty much everyone who called in was a woman. Almost no men called to feed their friends to the lions. Most intriguing of all was the fact that the women universally wanted fed to the lions their boyfriends, their husbands, or their male bosses. In other words, any man who held any sort of real power over women was, in the minds of the women who called the radio stations, an ideal meal for a hungry lion.

I spent a lot of time pondering the sociological implications of the response pattern. What did it mean that women wanted to see the men in their lives experience such a gory, albeit metaphorical, unpleasant fate? I was in the circus business, not the Sociology Department of a university, so I never pursued an real answers other than the fact that there seemed to be a lot of women in need of an outlet to vent about the men in their lives! I simply concluded that many women feel powerless around male coworkers.

Flash-forward to 2004 and the reality television show called *The Apprentice*, starring Donald Trump. At the conclusion of the first season, Trump was being interviewed on NBC TV. He was asked if there was anything surprising that he observed with the contestants, after all his years in business. Trump said that at the beginning of the show he made the two teams gender specific, with the women on one team and the men on the other; the women beat the men every time. When he changed the dynamic and mixed his two teams with both genders, the women became less assertive, less imaginative, and appeared to behave less powerfully. I found it amazing that nothing dramatically changed in 20 years . . . many women generally behave with less claimed power when working with men.

Here's how my radio promotion worked: I designed a thirty-second spot that opened with the sounds of lions roaring and cages rattling. Then the announcer would ask the listeners if they were fed up with someone currently in their life—a family member, an employer, or a friend. If so, the listeners were instructed to call in and win tickets to the circus by naming someone they wanted to feed to the lions. The call would come in and the listener would name the person he or she wanted to have fed to the killer cats, and describe, often in graphic detail, why that person deserved to be metaphorically devoured on the air. Once the person was named, you could hear the lions roaring again, cages rattling, then chewing, swallowing, and finally a belch! You could say that tastelessness never goes out of fashion. The spot was over, the tickets were won, the listener was satisfied, and no one was actually hurt.

I used that radio promotion over and over again. I felt honored when it became a stock promotion of the circus and sent out to all the other marketing directors. That bizarre promotion was one reason I won the Marketing Director of the Year Award in 1987, and received a bonus.

Engaging the public in a citywide promotion is a tricky job, especially in unfamiliar locations. There are certain issues, though, that are common to all people. One of life's commonalities is the fact that we all get our buttons pushed every day by people whom we allow to have power over us. We all need to blow off steam in a constructive way. When I designed this promotion, I wanted to allow people to have fun fantasizing about getting even with their button pushers.

Performance Tool: Idea Energy

I started this story with the concept that not everybody in a workplace is warm, fuzzy, and cuddly, and that there are in fact people with whom we have to work every day who could become a lion's lunch with little loss to the rest of the team. The concept of feeding your friends to the lions has an analogous location at the office, namely, the water cooler. People have been gossiping about coworkers at the water cooler since the time they first learned how to, well, cool water. In the Internet era, water cooler gossip often isn't enough for the truly disgruntled. These individuals actually turn to public websites such as www.vault.com or www.icered.com, which allow them to post unedited, unfiltered, unadulterated criticism of their coworkers and bosses. Job seekers, the media, and any other interested parties visit these websites to see exactly what people are saying about their employers. Frequently, what they are saying about their employers is not exactly the sort of thing that a company would want known about itself. So the question becomes: Is there a healthy and even useful way for employees to vent about people, places, practices, or rules without spreading the company's dirty laundry all over the global village?

The answer, surprisingly, is yes. There is such a way. Many businesses are now establishing anonymous Intranet websites allowing employees to post criticisms of their peers and of their bosses as well. These Intranet websites, which are not available to the general public, and exist within the firewall that protects all of the company's confidential postings, do in fact deter many employees from going public on vault.com, icered.com, or similar sites with their critiques of their companies. That's a positive. It's also a chance for people to explore their own thoughts without turning something into a formal negotiation or discussion between employer/employee and employee/coworker. The postings also enable all levels of management to have a stronger sense of how the cubicle dwellers really feel about each other and the brass. Companies are able to gain valuable personnel information, and often nip alcohol, drug, and potential relationship related problems in the bud, thanks to the information posted on these sites.

Any techie can build such a site into a company's Intranet. Someone has to monitor the postings to make sure that neither the company nor any individuals are liable for slander. You could call such a screener the "Vent Coordinator." But whoever is minding the store, this can be a very positive way of helping employees to blow off steam in a healthy manner while providing the company with much needed information about personnel.

Of course, if things get really bad, you could probably rent a couple of lions, and bring them to the cubicle of the offending party, but ultimately that might not be the wisest choice!

The serious point here is that people want and need safe ways of expressing their negative emotions about coworkers. No one wants their head bitten off, not even a lion trainer!

Win Emotional Juggling Matches

America is blessed with a multitude of small towns, but on an autumn day, for my money, Rustin, Louisiana is about as pretty as a town could be. The town is beautiful, quiet, and safe—the southern equivalent of a Norman Rockwell painting. The earth in Rustin is clay so red that I had to buy a special pair of red shoes to use, so as not to permanently change the color of my traditional blue and black pumps. The blood red soil of Rustin was new ground for our circus, as well. We had never performed west of the Mississippi, so I had the special challenge of introducing our circus to a town that had never known us before.

I liked the idea of the challenge. The entire state of Louisiana would be culturally different. And as virtually all of the cities we visited, I anticipated we would be welcomed. In any city, my role was to reawaken circus memories for those parents who had either heard of us or enjoyed the circus experience when they were young, and to acquaint their children with our circus, too. The circus had no history of prior goodwill on which to rely in Rustin. Everything was going to be brand new.

As soon as I arrived, I checked into the Best Western Hotel, which seemed to be the nicest place in town. I then went to the main post office to pick up my mail from General Delivery. The circus home office used the main post office in each town to send our mail and supplies for each campaign. These would include a binder of contacts, contracts, press releases, ad slicks (layouts of camera-ready artwork for print advertising), and each marketing director's personal mail. Everyone on the advance team would use the address of the home office in Deland, Florida as a temporary address for personal and business mail while we were touring. Our paychecks were sent to General Delivery, as well, with our marketing supplies.

I noticed my weekly paycheck wasn't part of the mail in Rustin, but I thought I'd wait a couple of days before I followed up. A couple days passed. I started the media and promotion campaign around town, and Rustin, it turned out, was just as receptive to the circus coming through as any other small town where we had ever performed. Things were going great. There was only one problem—I hadn't been paid.

I called the home office to report that there must have been some missing mail since my paycheck hadn't arrived. They told me that the circus wasn't doing well at the box office, since we were now west of the Mississippi River where we had little name recognition with ticket buyers. We moved by truck, as opposed to railroads, and could only afford to drive a few hours overnight to get to the next town and set up for shows in the morning. Cities west of the Mississippi were so spread out that truck shows from the east coast typically didn't travel west of the Mississippi, or they would lose days of business. The distance between towns would make it prohibitive. A tented circus must make money every day to stay in business. The fixed costs of feeding animals, buying fuel for generators, cooking for the performers and show personnel are the same whether you have shows that day or not. The bottom line: they didn't have the money on hand to pay me on time. Nor was I given the respect or the courtesy of discussing an alternate payment plan before the delay of the current paycheck.

This was a shocking development. I was young, and didn't have a lot of money saved, so my ability to go without a paycheck had a fairly short shelf life. Once I finished figuring just how many more days I could go without being paid, and it wasn't really that many, my innate sense of equality and fairness kicked in. "This wasn't right!" I took the position that the circus and I shared equally in this business relationship. I needed to earn money, and they needed people to promote the circus so that they could make money. My work effort was the key to the circus earning money in the towns I was assigned to promote. And I was good at what I did.

I firmly believed that it was the responsibility of the circus owner to infuse money into the show in order to make payroll when box office receipts were down. I understood that the show ownership was trying to expand it's market and grow the business, and that doing so was a risky proposition that might put a crimp in their cash flow. But I was not being compensated on a share the risk/ share the wealth basis. I was being paid a straight salary. It didn't seem fair to me that I should be asked to share in the risks, and go without a paycheck until their cash flow was stronger; they weren't planning on cutting me in on the rewards.

On top of that, I felt I knew a little bit about the circus owner. He owned a conglomerate of thriving businesses in addition to the circus and I felt he had the money to stem any cash flow crunch that the circus might have been experiencing. So I made the circus an offer. I would suspend services until they could send me my paycheck. I would drive to Dallas, a few hours from

Rustin, on a minivacation. All work in Rustin would have to wait until the circus caught up with the back pay it owed me.

I admit I held my breath for a moment or two as I awaited the circus' response. They could have fired me on the spot. Or would they have? It was an interesting test of Mental Chess and logic-driven positioning to see how this showdown was going to play out. I really didn't think beyond this point. I worked from the gut out. I only knew that I couldn't let my employer call the shots on something so important as paying me on time. So although the circus held the purse strings as my employer, I considered that we actually had a fairly equal amount of power. I always looked at my relationships with my employers as a supply and demand, a goods for services equation that was equally balanced.

Most people tend to mistake the money position in a relationship for the ultimate power position. Just because one side of the negotiating table has the money doesn't mean that the other side is powerless.

The circus responded that if I didn't keep working, we wouldn't be able to sell enough tickets to the show, and how could the circus succeed under those circumstances? The circus also mentioned that the other seven marketing directors in my department were agreeing to wait on their paychecks due to these tough circumstances. In other words, they were appealing to my "team player" sensibility, which was of course, quite strong.

My response: "Exactly." If I don't work, you don't sell tickets. In other words, we both have responsibilities. My responsibility was to work hard enough, long enough, and smart enough so that there would be great financial reward to the company. Their responsibility was to pay me for that work. I reiterated that I would wait in Dallas and call each day for the arrival of the paycheck. Then I would drive back to Rustin and finish the work. I headed to Dallas, where I had the time of my life.

On my first day in Dallas, I called the Best Western. "Any checks arrive for me?" The answer was "no." Ok, I thought, it's going to take them a little bit of time to start the wheels in motion.

Day two. Another call was placed to the hotel. Still no check. I went back to my partying in Dallas, but this time I couldn't escape the somewhat nagging feeling that maybe the circus had figured a way to do without me. I didn't like that thought at all, as I loved my job, I loved the circus, I loved the traveling, and I loved meeting people in towns around the country.

Day three. I called the Best Western Hotel. Was the check there? The answer was "yes." Was I enormously relieved? Yes, I was. I immediately drove back to Rustin to finish my advance work. We had a successful show date there. I juggled my way to the bank.

Performance Tool: Mental Chess

It turned out that a heartfelt, well thought out game of Mental Chess in Rustin, Louisiana encouraged the circus to realize the importance of keeping its payment obligation. I knew my value to the company. And in my quick calculations, I knew the value of the company to me. I definitely didn't want this issue of late payment to be a deal breaker that severed our relationship. This was my dream job. Yet, I just couldn't allow myself to be taken out of the decision-making process regarding something so important as my payment for marketing services.

Even though I knew the value of my work to the company, I didn't have an exaggerated view of my position. I mattered a great deal to them, but if they really needed to replace me they could have trained someone else for my job. It's intrinsic to the outcome of Mental Chess not to have a bloated sense of your own importance. That breeds arrogance and pride, and pride goeth before the fall. By knowing my value to the company, and my replacement cost, I knew how far I could take things with them in my round of Mental Chess.

It doesn't take a business genius on the order of Bill Gates or Warren Buffett to reach this simple conclusion: if you aren't getting paid, you aren't getting respected! Agreed? If you aren't getting respected, you aren't in an equally balanced relationship; your relationship is a little bit off kilter. The ultimate outcome of Mental Chess: the relationship is the winner. If the outcome ends your relationship, at the very least, you have reinforced your self-respect, your dignity, and your power of self-expression.

Up to this point, I worked hard to cultivate an equally balanced relationship with the circus. I loved and respected all of the people. They were exceptional, hardworking human beings. These were professional relationships that I appreciated and wanted to continue.

And they knew I worked hard to be good at my job. They knew that they could count on me, day after day, town after town. As a result, we shared an equal amount of respect for each other, translating into a balance of power. In the short term, they could not survive without great marketing directors. In the long run, of course, they could have fired me and replaced me with someone else. I understood that. But the cost of firing me, in financial, emotional, and legal terms, was far too high to justify because of a disagreement over the timing of my paycheck.

Employees and vendor/consultants who believe they are at the mercy of their employers or clients, are frequently underestimating the amount of power they really have in these relationships. The key for employees and vendor/consultants is to view relationships with employers and clients as relationships of equally balanced power, even if the authority in the relationship belongs to the employers and clients. By authority I mean the side that has bottom line decision-making in the relationship. In a two-party business relationship, one party has to make final decisions. That doesn't mean that that party has more power in the relationship than the other party. In this particular case of my paycheck held hostage, I felt the balance of power tip too far away from me. When it became a one-sided management decision to hold paychecks, I felt I had to move aggressively or lose my footing in the overall relationship, with long-term effects.

By cultivating an equally balanced relationship, you cultivate a flow of power. That power flow is important when sensitive circumstances force positions. The way you as an employee or vendor/consultant position yourself through your communication skills, the manner in which you strategize and respond, allows you to use your power judiciously, and successfully.

During that brief and unexpected emotional phone game of Mental Chess, the home office reminded me that I was breaking ranks with my fellow employees, the other marketing directors who were performing the same tasks that I was performing for the circus. I replied that my teammates, as much as I liked and admired them, didn't pay my bills. I was the only one who paid my bills. So don't let that "You're letting the team down" argument sway you. You're only a team as long as you are all being paid. Once they stop paying you, exactly what kind of team do you think you are on?

The lesson is this: no party has greater power over another party in any business relationship, as surprising as that may sound. Both parties share responsibility in the business relationship in order to make it succeed. Both share rewards. Once the relationship rules are defined and accepted, typically in the form of a contract, the balance of power is defined. This includes the power to change the rules or the terms of an agreement or contract. Once the rules are established, neither side has the right or the power to change terms unilaterally without approaching the other side with a request and a reason to change. The terms in a business agreement can only change, and the relationship can only stay balanced, if both parties change the terms together. If one party changes the terms, the other party is not bound to accept those changes. An exchange of business philosophy through a game of Mental Chess can be the best approach towards rebalancing the power.

I would add that I don't think I lost respect from the circus for being specific about the nature of the business relationship I was willing to accept. I didn't lose my job, thank goodness. I did risk that my decision to vacation until I got paid could have cost me my dream job. But I saw a greater risk—allowing myself to be powerless in future decisions with this employer, and further, with any employer who would change the terms of our relationship without consulting me. I didn't see that I had a choice if I wanted to maintain a balance of power in the relationship. In the end, everything worked out just fine.

If you are willing to use the Performance Tool of Mental Chess to keep your relationships on an equally balanced basis, no one can take ultimate control of your part of the relationship from you.

Innovation Rattles Cages

Right smack in front of the hot dog stand on the Midway of the circus, I met my future, short-term husband, Clarke Weigle. He was the circus euphonium player in their eight-piece brass band. I felt I knew him. Before long, we did fall in love and married. As a new bride, I wanted to live with my husband during our first year of marriage. That didn't seem like too much to ask.

From the company's point of view, this was not good news at all. It meant that I had to quit working in advance of the circus. The year previous, I took on a new role. My job had been to book the circus in cities six months to a year into the future. My job title was Contracting Agent. I functioned much like a location scout for a film shoot: I chose cities with specific pieces of property for performance, and partnered with nonprofit sponsors to support the circus appearance in every town we scheduled. The process of booking the circus in cities is called "routing the show," designing the tour schedule for the upcoming season. Not only did I have to quit a job at which I had been highly successful, I was quitting a job that no other woman had ever done. I was the first female contracting agent in the history of our circus.

Contracting agent was probably a male-oriented job because it meant constant travel without seeing any familiar circus people for months at a time, sometimes even for a whole season. Few women seemed to want to take on that sort of burden and solitude. The contracting agent had to find local non-profit organizations, which were comprised mostly of men, to sponsor the circus. Sponsoring the circus entailed obtaining rental rights for the property we would use for our show, making business introductions for us around town, and accepting part of the proceeds of our stay in their town as a donation. Cocktails and cigars in lounges "with the boys" typically followed a contract signing. So this really was something of a man's world.

I was not big on cigars and I didn't drink very much, but I sure did like to laugh. Who doesn't? So humor became my "cocktail du jour" when I was out with the boys. I never had a problem getting contracts signed, and the men I worked with never had a problem with my gender. Well, I guess I had done a good enough job that the circus was much angrier than I thought they would be when I told them I wanted to stay with Clarke and travel on the road *with* the performers.

The circus now had two problems: they had to get someone to replace me in advance of the show, and they needed to figure out what to do with me *on* the show. I further misread circus management when I presented them with what I 32 My Office Is A 3-Ring Circus! thought was the perfect job for me and for my unique situation—an advance person, a non-performer, working within the ranks of performers. With my talents and experiences over the past few years, I thought perhaps I could work as a liaison between show personnel and the marketing directors to improve efficiency with regard to media interviews, promotions, parades, and ordering dumpsters. I offered this idea to management. The circus had no desire to allow me to create a new position, one that I absolutely believed would be extremely useful. Right or wrong, I felt that they wanted to punish me for getting off the road. So they ordered me to become an elephant rider, a showgirl, and me with no athletic skills at all!

I thought I was offering some great solution to the question of how I could live with my husband during our first year of marriage and still serve the circus. But to the Powers That Were, I was something very different. I was the Bad Girl of the Big Top!

Now, maybe you were athletic when you were growing up. I wasn't. Gym class was a nightmare for me. I just had absolutely no athletic ability, and hardly any desire to develop some. What's a girl to do?

It was February 1985 and we were in winter quarters, in Deland, Florida, getting ready for the new season. Performers with animals were checking in. Roustabouts (circus labor crew) were returning from another tour, or reporting on other roustabouts who were lodged courtesy of the county in different parts of the United States, if you get my drift. Workers were polishing, repairing, and painting cages, trucks, and rigging equipment, in advance of our March opening.

I was fearful. Things weren't going according to my plan to create the job I wanted. On top of that, I fussed that I had been set up for failure as a performer. The problem was that although I could put on a red ping-pong ball nose and do radio and TV interviews with the best of them, I wasn't a performer. I was a businesswoman.

Talk about a need for crisis management skills! My reaction to the assignment of elephant rider—I hid in fear for three days. I literally hid in the bushes, avoiding the inevitable, but also studying the movements of the pachyderm, specifically the mounting and dismounting of the other elephant riders, the beautiful showgirls.

Most of all, I was fearful of just getting up *on* the animal! Ever looked at an elephant from the point of view of *riding* one? They're *really big*. The pachyderm helps the rider gain access to his body by crouching down on the ground and flattening his front legs. He is then available for the rider to step up on the joint of the leg and be flipped in the air. The elephant aims you so that if you have your legs spread eagle, you'll land around its neck. If that doesn't work, you'll either crash into the side of the elephant, or worse, fly across the top of the animal and land on the ground, on the opposite side.

Elephant riding is actually a fairly serious art. It's not the simplest thing in the world. Like many circus acts, elephant riding is a multi-generational family tradition. In our circus, a Native American man, his daughters, and even his granddaughters were the circus riders. There were three elephants and three riders to each of the three rings of our circus. When those girls got up on the performing beasts, they made it look so easy and graceful. It just wasn't easy, and certainly wasn't natural, for me.

There's more to riding an elephant than, well, riding an elephant. You've also got to be dressed appropriately. If you are a female elephant rider, you've got to be wearing a tutu with a ruffle. Like many women who had psychologically damaging experiences with tutus in their ballet classes at four years of age, I have never lost my pathological fear of tutus. Yes, the site of a tutu can send me screaming to a therapist's couch quicker than you can say "Here come the elephants!" Now, it's one thing to put on a tutu. It's another thing to put on a tutu and confront your tutu phobia. It's another thing altogether to clamber onto the leg of an elephant and have him flip you onto his shoulders while wearing a tutu. (*You* are wearing the tutu, of course, not the elephant.)

Ever feel an elephant's skin? It's rough, like wrinkled sandpaper. The hair of an elephant is incredibly scratchy and sticks straight up like long, pointy thorns. Let me tell you, a tutu is *no match* for the rough, scaly hair of an elephant, especially when you are getting tossed onto his shoulders at high speed. Elephant hair burn, when you're wearing only the briefest of costumes, is nothing to laugh about.

Okay, now it's day four and I emerge from the bushes. (Perhaps the bushes were chopped down to get me out; don't remember; exact details are a blur.) I'm in my tutu and ruffle. I've offered myself up to the elephant, and the elephant has successfully flipped me onto his neck. But we've only begun!

Now I had to learn to stay on the neck while the elephant walked around the ring for a few minutes. This is like nothing I've ever experienced. It's so much more intense than riding a horse. One elephant footstep launches an enormous wave of quaking motion, while the second footstep ensures that you will fall off if you don't hold the head bridle firmly and move in rhythm with its motion. They ought to make elephant riding an event at the rodeo! I was very lucky to stay on, and I still don't understand how I developed the coordination that it took to remain on that elephant's back for the five minutes that my career as an elephant rider lasted. It was the most agonizing five minutes of my life. In my mind, I was a fat lady riding an elephant, and that's not what I wanted to be. I wanted to be a businesswoman again. I wanted to get out of that tutu, and I wanted to get off that elephant's back, once and for all.

I got my wish. My elephant career ended. It was equally clear to the elephant trainer, myself, and probably, for that matter, the elephant that I was never going to cut it as a professional pachyderm princess. In exhilaration, I turned in my tutu. An elephant rider I would never be.

Does this mean the circus relented and allowed me to work at the position I had devised for myself? Not a chance. Instead, the circus gave me a different assignment that I suspected was also supposed to entice me to go back to working as a contracting agent. I was to be the Dancing Bear, a ground act that would neither endanger my life nor invoke the use of the circus' insurance policy and workman's compensation coverage.

If riding an elephant was terrifying, working as a Dancing Bear was initially humbling. I felt embarrassed in my new role. I was a bear with a college degree. The two concepts didn't seem to fit. I had to center myself every time I would suit up. The Dancing Bear in our animated animal act wore a heavy fur costume with a silver skirt around the hips, a large *paper mache* head, and danced to "Hava Nagila."

The circus seemed to be sending me a very pointed message, I thought. They really wanted me back on the road as part of the advance team. Flattered as I was, I couldn't relent. I was newly married and dedicated to the relationship.

So I became the best Dancing Bear they had ever known. I studied old Yogi Bear cartoons for their comic nature (this *was* a comedy animal act) and I learned to yell "yikes" with my hand swung behind me, placed over my butt, while in full throttle running, just like Yogi Bear. I learned to be "pleasant to the customers," even when children were attacking me thinking

I was some sort of action figure as opposed to a real live human being, a college-degreed businesswoman disguised as a Dancing Bear. Plus, I studied the actual live bears we had in the circus so that I could develop my character authentically.

Always a fan of inside jokes, I pushed the limits of performance in my animal act. Jimmy James, our ringmaster, the most perfect ringmaster of all time because of his commanding stature and bombastic voice, loved to laugh. And I loved to see if I could make him crack up on the microphone while announcing my act. At various times, I would come out with wardrobe accessories added to my bear costume, just to make Jimmy James choke. My favorite thing was to don a cape from the trapeze act, and wear it on my back. The metaphor: "Is the Pope Catholic; does the Bear poop in the woods?" To get back at me, Jimmy would order the band to play my show music triple fast, making it impossible for the huge *paper mache* head to stay in place on my shoulders!

When the circus saw that I wouldn't be thrown off course by their decision to assign me the Dancing Bear character, I knew I had won a personal battle to reinvent myself in a foreign environment.

The clowns all knew that I was trying my best to be the perfect Dancing Bear. One day, they plotted to challenge my acting ability by planting an older child in the audience as a participant in the comedy animal act. This particular act that included humans in the characters of gorilla, lion, horse, and giraffe, was devised as a vehicle for a media promotion and encouraged town children to write in to win an opportunity to be a "child animal trainer" for a day with the circus. Winners were given front row seats for their families. In order to participate in the act, the ticket winners donned ringmasters' coats and held small fake whips. When it was time for the animated animal act, the winners would be brought from the audience to center ring by the clowns. Each child, with clown attendant, would line up next to one of the fake animals, and upon cue from the ringmaster, would pretend to crack the whip while each animal stepped to the very center of the ring to perform our fake animal tricks.

One fateful day during the afternoon show, my "winner" cracked the whip aggressively, like he really meant to hurt me. It was hard to see out of the mouth of the bear's head to figure out what was going on. I felt the whip crack hard on me, even with the fur as protection. Being the true performing professional that I was, I felt I couldn't break character in center ring, in front of a full house, yet I wanted to respond to this act of violence. Calling on my method acting approach to performance, I used the persona of Yogi Bear that I had studied earlier in the season. I held my butt, like Yogi did when he thought he was on fire, yelped a bit, and ran out of the ring to end my portion of the act early and get away from this terror of a child. At the backstage performers' exit of the tent, I let hat kid have a tongue-lashing as soon as the other animals and the promotion winners came off stage! I told him exactly how I felt when he was cracking the whip at me that way.

I went into "red nose mode" after the 4:30pm show and considered that we had a long season ahead with clowns who periodically got bored. So I planned what I would do if the clowns set me up again. Can you guess what happened next?

I caught them, those rascal clowns. They thought they could fool me again at the 8pm show. My child trainer was . . . ? The same kid! And he's standing right next to me again! My worst nightmares realized; there was a plot going on. My plan B was formulated and ready to go. I had to stay in character, but I wasn't going to let the kid and clown have the upper hand. With the first note of "Hava Nagila," I came out of the animal formation roaring ferociously, squared my eyes on the child, and pretended to attack him like a cartoon wild bear, carrying him out of the center ring to the backstage area. I scared the pants off him for a minute, and it felt great!

Performance Tools:
Idea Energy, Crisis Avoidance

Upon arriving at winter quarters in February 1985 with my circus bandleader husband, Clarke, my plan was to reinvent myself. I thought I could still be a businesswoman traveling *with* the circus, instead of in advance of the show, and coordinating media relations between the marketing directors and the performers. But sometimes, we just don't get what we want . . . initially. Our first attempt at molding new career choices doesn't always work. What do we do when this happens, cut and run? Hardly.

When it became clear that I would have to perform as the Dancing Bear in order to stay employed *on* the circus, I made up my mind to be the best Dancing Bear in the history of the performing grizzlies. And I didn't do a half bad job. I was a bear with a plan. I figured I could hold out as circus bear for as long as it took until something better came along. Idea Energy being my constant companion, I decided to reinvent the bear character from its previous interpreter.

I could see that I was headed for a crisis in personal satisfaction in my new environment if I didn't change my attitude about not getting to design a special role for myself as liaison between the performers and the marketing team. Once settled in my job of Dancing Bear, my on-going goal became reinventing the character and expanding its function in the animated animal act. I used my love of humor to make the bear as thought provoking and funny as possible, thus adding even more comedy to the act. This played well to the audiences, while entertaining the circus personnel watching in the wings, too.

A circus season is really long with hundreds of shows. To relieve boredom, the clowns set me up in a practical joke with the overage boy whooping me hard during my portion of the act. I could envision the clowns plotting to make the Dancing Bear the butt of a joke *again,* possibly more embarrassing. So between shows that fateful day of the attacking child, I decided on a strategy, a plan B, so that I could remain in character while maintaining control over a child gone wild. Sometimes the key to Crisis Avoidance is really Passivity Avoidance. If I had remained passive, that kid would have harassed me in front of another throng of 3,500 people at the evening show, something I truly could not let happen. Nobody wants to be humiliated, even if the clowns think it's the funniest thing in the world; and certainly nobody wants to be harassed in public. At that moment, I recognized that if I were to remain passive, I would be in for another whooping. The events required that I take the situation in hand, and that I take that child in hand as well. Hey, it was either the kid or yours truly. How a fourteen-year-old boy could think that he could get away with beating up a bear twice in the same day means that he did not know I was "smarter than the average bear."

Passivity in the face of aggression is a ticket to failure. Sometimes we have to act, and act quickly, on our own behalf to avoid a crisis.

Never be ashamed to stand up for yourself, no matter who is cracking the whip.

Get Creative With Crisis

Frank Sinatra sang about it: "South of the Border . . . Down Mexico Way . . ." The composer, Leonard Bernstein, in his opera version of *Candide*, came closer to my own experience with a song lyric that said, "I'm Spanish! I'm suddenly Spanish!" Here's why.

Our circus was always looking for new markets into which to expand, and thought the Tex/Mex border towns might be good bets. After all, in the days when I worked for the circus, it was easy for Mexicans to come across the border into the United States to work, shop, or go to a movie. Crossing over the Guadalajara River from Nuevo Laredo, Mexico into Laredo, Texas at that time was as easy as walking across a city street. My upcoming assignment was Laredo.

So the circus eyed the potentially huge Mexican market, and it figured that more than a few Anglos would plunk down money for circus tickets in these border towns. I got the word that we would be testing out the border towns about six weeks in advance, and I decided to turn the experience into an opportunity for personal growth. I realized that I would be doing some of the promoting of the circus on Spanish language stations in Mexico. The circus instructed all marketing directors to hire translators to take us across the U.S./Mexican border towns, introduce us to Mexican business people, and generally help us promote the circus properly in another country, and in another culture. I didn't like the idea of letting a translator do all the work, though. Instead, I wanted to get the rust off my high school Spanish, in order to work with media and businesses in Mexico without a translator. Now that would be a great challenge, *si? Bueno!*

Our circus contained a number of Spanish speaking individuals, and I asked them to speak to me only in their language for the six weeks preceding my campaign in Laredo, even if I begged on bended knee for them to return to English. They complied, and by the time we got to Texas, I felt ready to do some of the Spanish language marketing work, like talking with the radio stations, organizing interviews for our Latino performers, and getting the print and TV campaigns ready to go in Spanish and in English.

Well, the great day came, and I walked across the US border into Nuevo Laredo. The translator I hired for my initial visits to Nuevo Laredo did a great job of introducing me to all the right media, and to some area businesses for cross promotions. I met the on-air radio disc jockeys, newspaper editors, and television hosts in those visits. With my translator, I made media buys on radio and television stations, and with the newspaper. I let my translator do much of the talking for me. After a couple visits to Nuevo Laredo with my translator, I found my way to the Nuevo Laredo Chamber of Commerce, and actually did my own spiel in Spanish. I needed the Chamber to hire Mexican residents to put circus posters up around town.

If I'd expected that six weeks of conversing with my fellow circus workers in Spanish would have me sounding like a diplomat, I guess I was wrong. Even with all the practice I could get, my Spanish was only somewhat better than it had been back in twelfth grade. It paid off, anyway. Some of the business people with whom I spoke were clearly touched by my effort to speak with them in their native tongue, instead of doing the "Ugly American" thing and assuming that everyone could understand English, especially if you spoke it loudly and slowly.

Interviews were arranged for our Spanish-speaking performers with media all over Nuevo Laredo. On opening day I would have transportation organized so that I could bring the hispanic performers south of the border to promote the show.

And that's where the trouble began.

Not a single Spanish-speaking individual from our circus displayed the slightest desire or intent to come with me to the interviews in Nuevo Laredo. Many of them had told me that they would be happy to cooperate in publicizing the circus in other towns. But now, when I definitely needed some espanol from the performers, every man, woman, child, clown, and acrobat of Spanish descent told me the same thing: they couldn't go.

The first excuses I got for the Mexicans' reluctance to cross the border didn't make sense to me. I knew it wasn't their actual immigration status, because the circus was extremely careful about hiring only people who were U.S. citizens or who otherwise had the right to work in the United States.

It took a lot more digging before I could get to the real reason why the Spanish—speaking circus performers wouldn't go south with me. Virtually all of them had heard stories about individuals of Mexican or Latin American descent, who were perfectly legal to live and work in the United States, who later revisited Mexico, and then were denied re-entry into the U.S.A. It didn't matter that these stories might have been completely false or that the subjects of these stories might in fact have been undocumented. The Spanish-speaking individuals in our circus simply didn't want to take the chance of failing to be readmitted to the United States, even though they had every right in the world to cross the border back into America. I had the sneaking suspicion that their families and friends might be crossing the border into Texas for some reunions and no media interview was going to ruin their fun. This still remains an unanswered mystery.

So they stayed behind, all of them. *Todos.* I was essentially left on my own to figure out a solution. I had to think quickly: I would be the subject of these interviews. There was no time to do anything else. I didn't mind terribly much, because I had had a fair amount of experience at speaking extemporaneously on American radio. Except I felt somewhat intimidated by my twelfth grade Spanish, at best. I was going to be broadcasting by myself in Spanish to a Spanish speaking audience that represented a huge potential of circus goers. This was a situation that strapping a red nose onto my face couldn't salvage! What else was I to do?

The show must go on, of course, so canceling the Nuevo Laredo media interviews was never an option. I decided to do the interviews myself and pretend to be a series of different performers. I explained the situation to each DJ and station manager awaiting our visit, and further explained that I did have a degree of conversational Spanish, but not much. So the announcers were to ask me questions about the circus in their language, and then interrupt me fairly quickly, so as to guard my ignorance from the listeners. The ploy worked. On every radio station where I did an appearance, the host would ask me a question, allow me to begin an answer, and then jump right in with an elaborate statement about our circus. Thus, I was able to say what I needed to say about the circus without compromising the secret that the listeners were not in fact listening to Madalena, the lion trainer, "Trabajo con los liones y tigres"; Sonya, the snake charmer, or even Rosario Del Mundeo, our Sideshow attraction with "the longest hair in the world." Our listeners thought they were getting to know all those other people, but the only one actually in the studio was yours truly.

Performance Tools:
Crisis Avoidance, Idea Energy

The crisis in the Laredo/Nuevo Laredo campaign was that I had Spanish-speaking radio stations expecting Spanish-speaking circus performers to be present for interviews so that we could promote the circus to Spanish-speaking circus goers. And for reasons only they could understand, none of the hispanic performers in our circus wanted to cross the border and fulfill the interview schedule I booked for them across the Guadalajara River in Nuevo Laredo, Mexico.

Crisis Avoidance was unknowingly engaged six weeks prior to the Laredo campaign when I gave myself a personal challenge. I wanted to see if I could work in the Spanish language in the towns along the Texas/Mexico border. Well, I found that I could when I approached storeowners and the Chamber of Commerce to display circus posters, south of the border. But when faced with having to speak Spanish over Nuevo Laredo radio, I had to improvise—I morphed into the characters of the lion trainer, snake charmer, and hair lady. As previously used in Panama City, Florida in "Clowning Around With Crises," Crisis Avoidance was employed prior to that fateful day when Bubbles was thrown out of my car. I was able to make a bold move like that because I had prepared to function somewhat as a performer with red noses tucked into the glove compartment of my car. If you are diligent about the practice of collecting information and knowledge in all facets of your work, while challenging yourself personally in the context of your work, you will be able to avoid most crises.

To perfect Crisis Avoidance you must get to a point where your basic expectations of yourself wildly exceed your employer's or your client's expectations of you. Your natural inclination should be to create personal challenges for yourself, like brushing up on Spanish before going to Mexico, even with an interpreter available; and to listen and act on sage advice, all of which will serve as your support system when you have to make on-the-spot crisis avoidance choices.

Then there are the daily basics of Crisis Avoidance. *First*, when you attend meetings, bring the whole file, not just the one or two documents you think you might need. There may be some doubt over a particular term of the deal. The last thing you want to be like is the clerk in a 99-Cents Store with his hand in the air, asking for a price check. *Second*, learn everything you can about the past and future projects of your client or employer. They will accord you respect, and future business, commensurate to your familiarity with their businesses. Plus, you'll be able to red flag problems as a result of your awareness and sensitivity. *Third*, show up early because being on time is too late if there are crises about to bubble. *Fourth*, if you are cell phone dependent bring an extra battery so that you are always reachable.

The easiest way to develop self-confidence with your Crisis Avoidance abilities is to conduct problem-solving exercises right now with issues at work. Develop plan Bs for snaffoos that could happen. You could become a hero when you least expect it. If our jobs don't get done, or don't get done correctly, then clearly we haven't performed to the best of our abilities, because few, if any of us are out there curing brain cancer. (Apologies go out to brain surgeons.) We're just trying to make the world a little bit easier, safer, more productive, or less expensive for our employers and clients. We're all up to the task of avoiding crises. Anticipate the worst; you'll reap the best rewards.

Idea Energy fuels reinvention. Three imaginary circus performers were created on the spot when the goal of fulfilling much needed radio interviews had to be resolved for Nuevo Laredo. When we can take dilemmas as intriguing challenges, instead of insolvable obstacles, we're on our way to running circles around our competition. Our bosses will love us for it, and our paychecks will reflect the efforts we make with the results we create.

There's an expression often heard around the National Football League: "There are no medals for trying." That may sound harsh, but it contains much truth. It didn't do the circus any good if I *tried* to have the interviews take place in Nuevo Laredo. No interviews and no promotion equal no ticket sales. The fact that "something went wrong" shouldn't excuse a serious person from accomplishing his or her tasks. Sometimes we have to be creative and find alternate means of getting the job done. The problem is that too many people have a mindset that says that failure is tolerable. Why should failure be tolerable? Why should we have such low standards for ourselves that we are willing to pass along crummy results to the people who are paying us good money to get good results?

Maybe it has something to do with living in an era when no one, from the President of the United States to many corporate CEOs, feels the need to take responsibility for their actions unless caught. We'd like to think that we are in the efforts business, and that as long as we give a good effort, all will be well. But the reality is that we live in the results business. We have to produce results, or our employer, if he or she has any brains at all, will replace us with someone who can.

Reinventions due to impending crises can be really fun. I had a blast doing those Mexican radio shows. The biggest obstacles can lead to the most creative thinking. Sure, stress creeps in when your plans seem to be unraveling before your very eyes. But if you can avoid succumbing to the stress and allow change to challenge your creativity, a big change can be truly enjoyable. At the very least, we always need stories for cocktail parties.

Avoid Pratt Falls

Children who are members of circus families lead different lives from the rest of the children in the world. Circus children travel from town to town with their parents, and are often part of the acts themselves. Whether they are performing or just along for the ride, circus kids move every couple of days to a new location, are frequently up late until the evening show is over, and everything has been packed away. They often dream of becoming circus performers in their own rights when they become adults.

Schooling is different for circus kids. Since they don't stay long enough in any one place to attend a traditional school, they either attend a "traveling school" composed of some teachers who marry into performer families on the circus and give classes to the kids, or their parents home school them. But for all the differences between circus kids and regular kids, all children have one thing in common. They all love Halloween.

Traditionally, the clowns would put on a special Halloween show, usually in drag, for the parents and the circus kids. The show would take place after the evening performance, around 11pm, in Clown Alley, a small tent within the circus village used as a dressing room for the clowns between acts. The clowns would arrange rows of seats around two sides of their tent, with standing room behind those seats. For circus kids, and for their parents, the Clown Halloween Show, in which the primary audience consists of the rest of the members of the circus, is one of the highlights of the year.

In 1985, the year I became the Dancing Bear, I took the Halloween Show to a whole new level. I combined the historic Clown Halloween Show with our Children's Theater Company of circus kids that I started because of my need to carve out a personal identity beyond work. I wanted to create unique work experiences for myself while traveling with the performers. I wanted to do more with the circus community than just my paid jobs of Dancing Bear and elephant ride ticket seller. With a theater company of circus kids I was also able to tap into a need that the kids had, an outlet for their individual creativity. The kids and I decided that for our big project as a theatrical troupe we would put on something truly special for all the other performers with the circus. I would direct the kids' show, and my then-husband, Clarke Weigle, the circus bandleader, would run the sound and lights for the production. The children wrote and arranged their own skits, and were as excited as could be about becoming the stars of the show with their parents as the audience.

The circus was in Naples, Florida, a small city on the west coast of that state. Halloween night was the opening night of a two-day run of performances. Our circus tent was a hundred and fifty feet wide by three hundred feet long, the length of a football field. The paying customers would enter through the main entrance or "front door" of the tent, while the back of the tent at the opposite end of the blue and white striped structure consisted of an enormous flap or "back curtain" that separated the inside performance space that the customers saw, from a large alcove on the other side. The "back curtain" was also known as the performers' exit, a place where the show people and their animals would congregate before they went onstage.

In Naples we pitched the tent in a huge open field with a row of tall, beautiful pine trees standing sentinel behind the "back yard" of the circus lot, the area behind the performers' exit, housing the wild animal cages. I was under the impression (where did I get this idea, anyway?) that there was a field behind those trees. No one actually checked. I just *assumed* there was a field that extended behind the trees. It turns out that there was a housing development on the other side of the trees with families and children of their own.

The skits in our special Halloween show were appropriately gruesome, visually and aurally graphic, using scenes from famous plays, stories, and music videos. One skit was a remake of the "Thriller" video, which was very popular at that time. If you remember back to the mid 80's, you saw Michael Jackson and a whole crew of once dead dancers, prancing cadavers, and all manner of things to terrify. Perfect for a Halloween night.

We also had cool props, like the lion trainer's gun that shot blanks, and excellent music to reinforce the emotional wallop of each skit. Performances included blood curdling screams, blowing wind, organ music, and lots of your basic Halloween noises.

The show opened with the three witches of *MacBeth* performing their ghastly and frightening opening scene of that play. They were in full makeup and costume. Anyone in earshot, who didn't know that it was simply circus performers entertaining each other, might have mistaken Shakespeare's words for the sort of pagan rituals that some people associate with Halloween.

Among the people who made that unsurprising mistake: some of those families in that development behind the row of pine trees. We were about to be in deep trouble, but we had no idea.

The show continued, to the delight of its audience and to the consternation of the neighbors. Police were on their way as our head clown, Sandy, concluded the first act with an outrageous rendition of Aretha Franklin's mega hit "Freeway of Love." Sandy was wearing a dress made from pages of an Atlas road map stapled together like a 1960's high-fashion cocktail dress. While Sandy gyrated to "Freeway of Love," the police poured in, found me, and told me that they were shutting down the show.

Why, I wanted to know. It turns out that the neighbors, of whose presence we hadn't suspected, heard all the gunshots from the graveyard scene, and the soundtrack of devil creature noises that we played for another skit. They didn't know what we were doing, but they assumed the worst, that we were performing some sort of evil rituals, behind the circus tent. After all, who knew what kind of people circus performers were? The clapping and cheering must have thrown them off, or maybe they thought that we were just extremely enthusiastic devil worshippers.

You couldn't really blame the good people of Naples, Florida. After all, our show had begun close to midnight on Halloween night, because our regular circus performance ended at ten and we needed a little time in order to prepare for the special insider's Halloween show.

The police saw otherwise, and ordered me to cut the power on "Freeway of Love" midway through the song. They charged the circus with disturbing the peace and a variety of other complaints, and they added some charges against us for keeping minors from being in bed at an appropriate hour. Obviously the police in Naples, Florida had little knowledge of the lives of circus kids, who followed a different clock than regular kids.

I tried to bargain with the police to let us finish the second half of the show quietly, without any sound effects. No dice. We invited them to stay. They didn't want to stay. We explained as best we could that circus life worked on a slightly different timetable than did town life. They didn't buy that, either. We pleaded special dispensation for a holiday; we pleaded entertainment deprivation . . . always entertaining the masses, and never being entertained ourselves. Not a single argument worked. We called curtains and packed up for the night. The circus kids were disconsolate. They never got to finish their show.

The next morning, I went to the circus office, a trailer that doubled duty as box office ticket wagon in the hours before performances. I had to meet with the owner of the circus himself, Johnny Pugh, a benevolent manager and a former flying trapeze artist. (Just to be accurate, Johnny was not the owner I referenced in "Win Emotional Juggling Matches.") He had the police report in hand, along with the fine he had to pay for our disturbance of the peace. He appeared to be mad, but I think he secretly liked the excitement. He reminded me that when I asked for his permission to use some circus property to stage the show, and to use the back of the main tent to present the show, I promised to keep everything orderly and trouble free. But I hadn't been thorough. I had angered, and disappointed, Mr. Pugh.

Yet as much trouble as I had caused the circus by not looking behind those pine trees, I had a strong, strong feeling that the show had to go on. We still had to perform that second half. Many of the kids in the show had their only numbers after intermission, and it would have been devastating to them had they never had the opportunity to strut their stuff. Fortunately, there were no graveyard scenes or sound effects in the second half. I then lobbied for us finish the show in Boca Raton, Florida, our destination the next day after leaving Naples. Johnny Pugh was amazing. He said "yes."

But not right away. First I got the verbal spanking I deserved.

"Judy, how could you do this to me?" Johnny wailed. "I tried to help you. I got you the generator for power. I allowed you to use company circus props. How could you let this happen? You told me that it would be quiet and there wouldn't be any trouble. Now we've got this costly embarrassment on our hands."

I immediately took responsibility, because it was the right thing to do, and because I knew Johnny was expecting me to do nothing less. "Listen," I began. "It's all my fault. I didn't look behind the tree lines. I didn't think about the fact that regular people go to bed, even on Halloween night, by midnight, when we were having our performance start. I accept full responsibility for this. I'll pay the three hundred dollar fine from the city. You know I'll take care of everything."

Johnny looked visibly relieved. "Thank you," he said. "That makes me feel better. I just hope you'll be more careful next time."

That's when I played a little game of Mental Chess. I knew that his moral core as a circus man was summed up in the phrase "the show must go on." And I also knew that he felt a sense of obligation to treat everybody in the circus family fairly, from the performers to the roustabouts, to the circus kids.

So I leaned in. "Well, there's still a second half of the show that we have to perform."

Johnny couldn't have been more surprised if I'd swung at him with a foam hammer. "You're not asking me to do the second half of the show, are you?" he asked.

What could I do? I shrugged. "Yes," I implored, "many of the kids didn't get to do their acts. You and I are childless, but we have to be sensitive to the feelings of the children here at the circus. And the show must go on, right?"

Johnny was rolling his eyes, but he wasn't saying no.

"I promise that *this* time, when we do the second half of the show, the volume will be lower. No screams. No gunshots. We'll do it earlier, and inside the tent instead of outside, so that nobody is disturbed. I'll act more responsibly, you'll see."

His response: "I can't believe I'm saying yes."

It took a fair amount of word play to get him to say yes. After all, I had just gotten the show in trouble with the police. I had triggered the levying of a fine against the circus; never a great thing to do. So I was probably not Johnny's favorite person at that very moment. Yet, I think he liked my chutzpah pushing on for the remainder of the show.

I had to use every argument I could think of. I told him that I would take up a collection at the performance that night to pay for our legal fees, and that I would personally guarantee that nothing disruptive or disorderly would happen at the special performance of the second half of the show.

The next night, in Boca Raton, the show went on, to the delight of the kids who got to perform their acts, and to the delight of the entire audience of circus folks. There were no untoward events, and peace and harmony between Johnny and myself was reestablished.

Performance Tools:
Mental Chess, Idea Energy

In order for the Children's Theater Company to perform that second half of the Halloween Show, after being shut down by the Naples, Florida Police on Halloween night, I had to play a very strong game of Mental Chess with Johnny Pugh, my employer. If I could sum it up in a phrase, I would say this: "Don't cower. Use your power!" Yes, Johnny was the owner of the circus, and I was an employee. But because I had done my work at the circus so well, I was respected, and I had made myself valuable to my employer. As such, I considered I was in an equal balance of power relationship with Johnny.

The following is a concept that is so very important to remember, and integral to every business relationship you have: you are always in an equal balance of power with your employer or client. You have to remember that and call upon its inherent strength when locked in verbal combat. We so often look at power in terms of job titles and salary levels. Johnny could not have done an effective job of running the circus, unless I did mine. We both grew to understand this balance of power concept better as we spent more time working together. Instead of approaching Johnny as an unworthy subordinate, I was able to continue to have discussions with him that stretched relationship boundaries. I felt comfortable using creative support reasons for my request to perform Act II of the Halloween Show in Boca Raton, like, "The show must go on."

The only person who can truly make you feel powerless is you! As long as you remember that you have just as much power at the negotiating table as anyone sitting there, you'll be fine. You've got more power than you realize. And when you use the Performance Tool of Mental Chess to negotiate, you demonstrate awareness of your power. As much as possible, always play to a win/win outcome for the relationship, as well as to a winning outcome for the specific issue at hand.

Idea Energy was engaged when the Children's Theater Company was created. You can carve a niche for yourself even in the smallest of business communities, like the circus. Selling elephant ride tickets and being the

Dancing Bear eventually became fun, but I still needed a role and function for myself that contributed to the circus community beyond my paid jobs. So I started the Children's Theater Company, reminiscent of my youth when I organized my sister and our friends to put on musical shows in our garage for the neighborhood families.

Everyone knows the expression, "The sky's the limit." In reality, for most people, the "I" is the limit. In other words, people place more limitations on themselves than any outside force ever could. We're governed to a startling degree by the opportunities we see around us, and by the skills and talents we choose to use. There are times when we have to compromise and make the best of a work situation for a short period of time. You can offset that compromise by creating something else that's valuable and fulfilling in that same work environment. You can use Idea Energy to augment your personal life or your role with the company if you can't get the job you really want immediately.

The only thing that stops people from adding more responsibilities to their jobs, taking on new endeavors, or new training for greater power, is fear driven complacency. Idea Energy forces us to take responsibility for the fact that we can grow in any environment by simply redefining ourselves. The "I" shouldn't be the limit. Only the sky should be the limit.

Career Wanted, Dead or Alive

The story that I'm about to tell you may sound like an urban legend. I understand. There are some things about circuses that seem too incredible to be true. But I can *almost* absolutely guarantee that this story happened. Not with our circus, but with a circus whose name, as I'm sure you will understand, I am not able to reveal.

This story involves a hippopotamus and a lot of luck. A hippo is the essence of relaxation and inaction. They don't do all that much. They hang around and mind their own business. Nobody wants to see hippopotami (the correct plural) if they're interested in action.

People go to circuses, though, not just for the excitement of the acrobats and the danger of the wild animals, or to see a man shot out of a cannon. A lot of times, people want to go to the circus because they know they will see the largest, ugliest, heaviest, or some other superlative-bearing creature, either human or animal. Some people like the animal acts. Some people like the acrobats. And some people *really* like the Sideshow. This is where the hippo worked.

Our circus traveled with a bona fide Sideshow, such as you would expect from a respectable traveling circus. Ours included a fat man, an electric lady, a contortionist, monkeys, and a petting zoo. The rival circus at the heart of this story had a Sideshow that also had a giant hippopotamus. Well, this circus was almost at the end of their touring season when one of the animal trainers began to think that their hippopotamus was getting sick.

Since hippopotami don't tear it up, it takes a little longer to tell whether a hippopotamus is sick. Except if you're a hippopotamus connoisseur. I don't think there were many on that circus. It apparently was very hard telling a healthy hippopotamus from an unhealthy hippopotamus.

Or an unhealthy hippopotamus . . . from a dead hippopotamus.

This is what had befallen our to-remain-nameless competitor circus. Their giant hippo, the star of their Sideshow, had gone to that great tub of water in the sky. It was no more. It was a circus . . . with a dead hippo. A dead hippo traveling.

A giant dead hippo is a giant live problem for a circus. You can't just put it out for garbage pick-up on Tuesday. You can't take him to the town dump. And no one yet has figured out any uses for a recycled hippo. Just as there are very stringent laws in our society about the disposition of dead human bodies, laws about the disposing of dead large animals are equally strict, and for the same reasons. A large dead animal is a health risk, whether left behind by a circus, buried, dumped in a river, or otherwise abandoned. It may be okay for somebody to leave a rusting mattress frame or even a Volkswagen by the side of a river. But a dead hippo? Don't even think about it. You've got to dispose of it properly.

After all, it's not as if dead hippopotami are easy to hide. They're not. As a circus veteran, you can trust me on that. If a dead hippo were to suddenly turn up in a town where the circus has just gone through, you wouldn't need a crack team of investigators to figure out that that recently departed hippo might once have belonged to that recently departed circus.

What do you do with a dead hippo?

Legally, you have to take it to a properly zoned area or back to your circus's winter headquarters, which is usually zoned both for the presence of live large animals and the burial of dead ones. You can take your dead hippo back to where you came from, and give him a proper send off there.

There's only one problem. If you're going to get a dead hippo to the winter headquarters, you can't call UPS. Or FedEx. Or even the Postal Service.

Nobody wants a dead hippo, not even in a box with stamps on it and a return address.

The only way to get a hippo to winter headquarters is to put him in a truck and take him there. That's what our rival circus would have done, but for one slight complication.

No spare trucks. They were a couple weeks away from the end of the tour, and from their winter quarters, but every truck was needed.

Make that two complications: no spare drivers, either.

A circus is a very tightly run enterprise, and there are simply no employees hanging around, doing nothing, waiting for dead hippos to transport across the nation. If you were to take a truck and a driver out of the mix, you would be unable to ship some of the live components of your circus to the next destination. The circus would have had to spare a truck and a driver for a week, even if they made all the red lights, in order to get that dead hippo to a legal and safe burial plot.

It was time to improvise. What do you do when you've got a large hippo, a now large dead hippo, and no way to get that dead hippo off your hands?

The answer: you do nothing. You simply keep the dead hippo in the act.

And that is what the other circus did. In the Sideshow, the hippo had been displayed in a huge vat of water. People paid good money just to see such an enormous animal up close. The Sideshow Barker merely changed his patter, as men and women, and boys and girls entered the Sideshow and were confronted with a motionless hippo, the hippo few of them would have suspected was no longer among the living. "As you can see," the Sideshow Barker would say each day, "the hippo is asleep. But if he were awake, he would be looking at you and thanking you for coming to this fine circus. Now if we can move along quickly to the other amazing thrills we have for you today, we can let our dear friend get some sleep. Because you know even our large animal friends need to sleep." It's hard work traveling in the circus, what with all that has to be done to prepare a fabulous and exciting show every day.

The key word in the Barker's patter was, of course, *quickly*. If a group of otherwise credulous adults and children are given only a brief amount of time to ponder a motionless creature, they are not likely to suspect its true health status. For all the circus customers knew, the hippo really was sleeping. Only the Sideshow Barker and the rest of the circus knew the truth.

All went well for our rival circus with its dead Sideshow attraction for the next couple weeks. They would spray it with some type of fragrance to keep it smelling fresh. By the last few days of the tour, the hippo had to be pinned together because the decomposition process had in fact begun. The hippo was breaking up into pieces. The funniest part of this story was that the Sideshow Barker would sometimes insist on silence for the hippo, so that he could sleep peacefully. Little did the viewers know just how peaceful that sleep truly was.

I'm going to leave you suspended in disbelief now as to the validity of this dead hippo story as an urban legend. If you catch me in one of your towns on a speaking engagement, I might just put the legend to rest. Unless and until that happens, you'll just have to take my word for it.

Performance Tool:
Idea Energy

Talk about an outrageous example of Idea Energy! It sure was the case when the beloved hippo almost became a liability. A different performance analysis of the hippo kept the mammal in play for the last couple weeks of the season. Sometimes we really do have to innovate under stressful circumstances. The circus could not have endured the loss of a man and a truck, nor would it have been possible or affordable to find a trucking company willing to ship such an unpleasant cargo. Trying to figure out how to get by without that truck and driver was not possible. There are minimum staffing limits in every department, below which it is simply impossible to go.

Idea Energy can be achieved through a solution that is literally right under your (red) nose. Sometimes a little sleight of hand is the only choice. Was the rival circus breaking any laws? Well, they were stretching the truth a little bit by describing the hippo's condition as one of temporary rather than eternal rest. But that's show business. At times, a little bit of exaggeration is necessary in order to avoid a bigger problem down the road.

The story did have a happy ending, at least for the hippo. I understand that he made it in one piece to winter quarters, where he was buried, with full circus honors, in a brief and touching ceremony. Rest in peace, sweet hippo. Thanks to you, the show did go on!

How about your show, your career? Is it lying in a tub of infected goals and dreams? Are you draining the life out of your spirit and snoozing through each workday? Perhaps it's time to bury your present job and move on to something that will add depth and purpose to your life. When you get to a point in your career where you're just treading water, you're in critical danger of losing control of your destiny; you can't contribute to society unless you are displaying your skills and talents properly.

Avoid this type of career crisis by using your mental energies to resurrect ideas that you may have been harboring for years. Successful and happy people try a variety of things before they define and redefine the right work for themselves. It takes time and perseverance to have a fulfilling life of fabulous careers. Don't water down expectations of yourself and of what life has to offer. Do the best you can with whatever work you have now; make the best of your current job situation while revving up for the next big career adventure.

Got Net?

Are you working without a net?

One of the most exciting moments in any circus performance comes when an acrobat performs on the high wire . . . without a net below. The audience is utterly still. Even small children, whose attention spans are not fully developed, recognize the gravity of the moment. Adults know exactly what's going on should the performer slip up; he is likely to fall to his death. Any individual willing to perform without a net, and thus risk everything on a single false move, commands our full attention and respect.

We had a high wire walker and high wire motorcyclist in our circus named Tabak. He was a great guy with a wonderful family. Tabak's wife home-schooled their children, who grew up to be intelligent, mannerly, sweet people themselves. It just so happened that they had a father who walked and motorcycled across a high wire for a living. But in the circus, that's just what people do!

Tabak performed two acts that were total crowd pleasers, and he worked without a net in both cases. In a tented circus, the audience is amazingly close to the performers. When Tabak performed, the audience would be right under the high wire. Teens especially loved Tabak's high wire motorcycle act, because it was noisy, flashy, and a symbol of rebellion.

The circus performers actually encountered few accidents. They all supervised their own rigging when the roustabouts were helping to set it in place with each new tent raising, in each new town. The circus performers were also well practiced at their trade and were extremely athletic. But every once in a while, things happened. That's the nature of live performance. They didn't think about it when they were performing, but each performer knew they had to go to an alternate career if fate changed the course of a dangerous circus career.

Such a fateful day came for Tabak while we were performing in Knoxville, Tennessee. Tabak was in the throws of his motorcycle act and the crowd loved it. Suddenly, a stake post that secured the low end of the inclined wire came loose. It had rained in Knoxville for days before the circus arrived, and the ground was too soft and moist to hold the stake in place. But we only found that out during the performance. In the middle of the act, the wire lost strength and Tabak fell onto a stake post that unfortunately inserted itself right up his derrière!

The good news is that Tabak survived the accident, which was witnessed by several thousand circus goers. Tabak's injury made clear to him that it was time to leave the circus and do something else. He didn't have a formal plan in mind for the day that he would have to stop performing, because like most of us, the unthinkable was something he just didn't want to think about!

Fortunately for Tabak, though, he had long been perfecting an avocation that he could turn into a career. He loved to cook. Tabak and his family left the circus, and Tabak quickly became a private chef in Florida. Before long, he opened a restaurant, which to this day is very successful. He is happy, healthy, and financially wealthy. Even when he was working without a net in the circus, he was fortunate enough to have unwittingly developed a safety net for his post-circus life.

Performance Tools:
Idea Energy, Crisis Avoidance

Working without a net is expected for circus performers. It ended Tabak's circus career when he fell from his high wire motorcycle in Knoxville, Tennessee. And it's certainly career suicide for the rest of us. It's really amazing how many people in our society have absolutely zero long-term planning going on. For all too many of us, our short-term goal is noon and our long-term goal is midnight. Anything beyond the current twenty-four hours is far too abstract for us to imagine. That's where Idea Energy comes in. Developing Idea Energy can help transform a potentially devastating change in your work life into a new career. Your safety net can be your use of Idea Energy, not only when unexpected dramatic change happens, but even while things look secure. A good practice is to develop safety net options for career choices while in the midst of your current career.

Worldwide, circus performers are rewarded for their courage and bravery by working without a net. For the rest of us, such a practice is usually disastrous, and there is no one to applaud. It is a given that our industries and our goals change throughout our lives. Technology forces people out of one job and into another. Generally, we catch the technology swell on the back end of the revolution, rather than anticipate the change with a new approach to our work.

We live in an era when entire industries become extinct. In the 1940s, it was said that if you wanted a secure and steady job for the rest of your life, you went to work for the railroads. But I don't think a single graduate of any MBA program in the country is thinking railroads when he or she leaves business school. Obviously things change, and in an era of enormous technological transformation, things change quickly. But not so quickly that we cannot see changes coming.

The whole idea is not to be taken by surprise by societal and technological change. If half the people in your department have lost their jobs over the last few years, and if your industry is getting thinner and thinner, then I would call it "working without a net" to show up at work every day without a contingency plan at-the-ready. If your job went away, if your company went away, if your industry went away, would you have a plan? Would you know where you would go next for work? Are you aware of other skills and talents you have that can be converted into a career? If you cannot answer that question in the affirmative, then you really are working without a net.

Most people live without any sort of financial safety net, either. If the average individual lost his or her job, what kind of financial resources would that person be able to draw upon before a financial crisis developed? Our society is geared not toward saving but to spending, and many of us spend up to, or even beyond, the limits imposed on us by our salaries. Few of us leave any money in the bank for the proverbial rainy day. Be creative about the way you handle your money. Crisis Avoidance can help in this area, too. You can make small investments that can be leveraged for quick money. Saving five dollars a day can add up quickly as a nest egg.

Since most people don't have much in the way of savings, we better not lose our jobs! Or disaster could overtake us with astonishing speed. Just think of all the Porsches and BMWs that were repossessed in Silicon Valley after the fall of the dot.com industry. Where are the drivers of those expensive cars now? What kind of financial safety net had they created for themselves?

These are uncomfortable questions. Most people don't want to confront these issues for the same reason that people don't want to buy life insurance: we just don't want to think that the worst could happen to us. We may be unique human beings, but we certainly are not above reality. Unfortunate things do happen in the business world, such as one's job, company, or industry going away. The good news is that industries do not disappear the way that dinosaurs did, with a meteorite exploding into the side of the earth, suddenly wiping out entire species. Just as success leaves clues, so does impending change. If we are paying attention to what's going on in the world, it might not come as a surprise to us that things could change, taking our jobs with them.

In other words, while I love watching acrobats perform without a net, because of the excitement and fear such courage generates, I'm not sure at all that such an approach is appropriate for one's career or personal finances. This is why I always ask the people I counsel: How do you practice Idea Energy and Crisis Avoidance in your career and in your financial life? Do you know what you would do if your job, your company, or your industry went the way of buggy whips of the late 19th century, or the dot.coms of the late 20th? Where would you go? In other words, what's your safety net?

Change is inevitable, so it's best to prepare for it instead of allowing it to overtake you by surprise. Just as it's easiest to look for a job when you already have one, it's easiest to determine your next career while you are still at work in your current one. Rather than postponing any thought of the future simply because it's too uncomfortable to think about, it really is essential for us to ponder these questions: What would I do if a meteorite hit my industry? Am I working without a career net? How long could I hold out if my salary went away? How quickly could I establish myself in a different field, if I had to? What sort of training, experience, or knowledge should I be acquiring right now, before the meteorite hits? Does my long-term planning extend past midnight tonight? Am I mentally ready for the challenge?

Human beings work on a pleasure/pain principle. We want to do the things that give us pleasure, and we want to avoid the things that bring pain. It is painful to think about preventive maintenance for our own future. It's much more pleasant to just assume that everything is going to be all right. But we all know that jobs, companies, and even industries don't last forever. Crisis Avoidance means doing the preparatory work now, so that if we had to act quickly and use Idea Energy, we would be in a good position to make the leap.

Got a career net?

Appreciating a Horse of a
Different Color

A circus truly is a traveling city. It consists of a community of people who live together in separate trailer homes, who shop at the same traveling store the circus maintains for the necessities of day-to-day life for the circus employees, who eat in the same outdoor dining room known as the cook tent, and who share a garbage pick-up service. The circus has a food concession truck where the residents can get hamburgers, hotdogs, and the other sorts of fun food that circus fans enjoy. The circus doesn't have a gas station, but there are fuel trucks that come to the circus in each town and fill up all the trucks and trailers throughout the week. And there's plenty for kids to do. Boy, are there pets! Lions, tigers, bears, chimpanzees. When the customers aren't around, the circus is one great big petting zoo for the performers' kids. Those lucky children also get to play with the moon bounce, and all the other attractions that children in the customers' families have to pay for.

For better or worse, the circus also has a fairly stringent caste system. The top tier employees include the advance team of promoters and contracting agents who travel ahead of the circus and live exclusively in hotels. Then there are the ticket sellers, the accountant, the operation manager, and the owner, all of whom travel with the circus and have their office in the back of the ticket wagon. You've also got the department heads and managers of each of the branches of the circus that include the animal acts, acrobatic acts, and the band.

The middle class, if you will, consists of the performers.

The circus also has the equivalent of a traveling working class. These are the roustabouts, the individuals who do all the hard work necessary to make a circus happen. The roustabouts are the ones who erect and disassemble the tent, put up banks of seats, install the circus rings and rigging, and generally do all the hard work that is required to allow the show to function. The roustabouts keep to themselves, for the most part. These are individuals who may have had troubled pasts, perhaps a troubled present, which they have joined the circus in order to escape. They may be with the circus for a very short amount of time, although some stay for years. Since the white-collar workers and the performers rarely mingle with the roustabouts, the roustabouts are perhaps the least-known group of individuals who travel with the circus.

By now, you know me. Arbitrary restrictions regarding whom you should and should not talk, or spend time with, carry no weight with me. I was curious about the roustabouts. I wanted to get to know them, so I made it my business to do so. I decided that I would actually join them in their work and get to know them better. Jail sentences aside, there were some very intelligent, moral, philosophical and well read men inside those red jumpsuits that they all had to wear. I talked about literature with several of them. It was quite surprising at first to find engaging conversationalists among this group of circus personnel, many in dire need of dental care. The roustabouts were commonly considered rather dangerous men whose trailer truck, a dormitory on wheels, if you will, was parked in the circus back lot where the other dangerous animals, lions, tigers and bears, were kept.

I had no idea what hard labor was until I decided to put on a red jumpsuit myself and join the roustabouts in their work. It was exhausting to help out with the assembly and disassembly of the circus tent in each new location, but I enjoyed pressing myself to work in this physical manner. I had never done anything like it in my whole life. It made a positive change both in my figure and in my self-confidence. And getting to know these ostracized young men, upon whom the circus was totally dependent, made it worth the experience of breaking all my nails.

Who among us ever discovers what his or her true limits really are? It's very rare for any of us to push ourselves in unexpected directions, to find out just what we are made of. This is the attraction of programs like Outward Bound, or vacations spent white water rafting instead of sitting around a beach at a resort with a cocktail in one's hand (not that there's anything wrong with that!). Life will afford us many intriguing opportunities to find out what we are made of, if only we will avail ourselves of those opportunities. I discovered that I had a capacity for physical labor that I never knew I possessed. I had the pleasure of dropping off to sleep exhausted from really hard work, and knowing that I had never been in better shape in my life. Above all, I saw myself in a completely new light. I saw that I was capable of doing much more than I had ever realized.

The same is true of the roustabouts. Although most had experienced levels of societal failure prior to their circus careers, they were able to stretch and grow in this environment that offered opportunity to those who wanted to better themselves and were willing to work hard for it. Much like the United States, the circus was an open environment that allowed people to tackle responsibility, achieve career growth and personal dignity, and work through the caste system to a higher level.

Performance Tool: Idea Energy

The roustabouts, circus laborers, are perfect examples of people who reinvented themselves with a lot of Idea Energy. Some of the roustabouts arrived at the circus in fairly disheveled condition, and yet many of them rose through the ranks of laborers to become department managers, staying with the circus for years. They either didn't have the opportunities in life that many of the rest of us had, like a stable home, an education, and social and business connections; or, they blew opportunities that could have turned into better lives for themselves. Under the encouragement of circus impresario Johnny Pugh, a truly respected leader and manager of people, they grabbed an opportunity when it arrived and made something wonderful happen for themselves.

In my personal learning experience with the roustabouts, it was a little different. Sometimes reinventing ourselves doesn't tie in specifically with a career move, the quest for a promotion, or the plan to merit a raise. Sometimes we want to push ourselves just for the sheer joy of seeing what's inside, of discovering that our limits are far higher than we could possibly have known. That's part of how I used Idea Energy when I lived in the circus as Dancing Bear and elephant ride ticket seller. In this case, I wanted to challenge my ability to accept people who were considered outcasts of society, and research what made them tick. The way I did that was by participating in the grinding work that the roustabouts performed—physical work that challenged me on a different level—I helped with tent raising, rigging, and tear down.

I also understood the human desire to seek comfort in terms of socializing strictly with "one's own." I questioned why we had to accept such a narrow definition of the term "one's own." I weighed my college education against work as a physical laborer. Not so curiously, I became svelte as a result of participating in the roustabout's work, a reinvention I gladly welcomed. Very surprisingly, I found that many roustabouts were avid readers, and between shows I had discussions about literature with those men in their recreational time.

The sad fact is that we stratify ourselves far too much in society. We don't look at ourselves as members of the same family—the human family. Instead, we are far too quick to write people off because they don't have our level of educational attainment, and because they don't look or think like us. (Much needed dental work and bad haircuts were part of roustabout fashion.) My combined experiences of talking literature with the roustabouts and carrying heavy tent poles taught me that educated people can take themselves far too seriously and can miss a lot of the wonder that is out there in the form of the less privileged sect of humanity.

By redefining the boundaries of who we are and what we think we can do, we become broader and better people. This sort of experience will be reflected indirectly in our employment conditions and salaries. How can it not? We're here to serve, and the more people to whom we can relate is proportional to the effect we can have in our jobs.

Ultimately, we are compensated to the exact degree to which we are useful to our fellow humans. We can infuse Idea Energy into reinventing our society one roustabout at a time.

Call the Shots in Your Show

The Sideshow is a world unto itself within the circus. The circus, as we have seen, is a microcosm of society at large, with a caste system similar to that found in American society. Within the Sideshow, you find many of the same individuals who, in a greater society, would locate themselves at the margins. These are the highly unusual performers, either because of their physical attributes or because of the unique skills they have developed.

Typical attractions at Sideshows include an electric lady, contortionist, pin man, and, of course, a fat man. The Sideshow is located on the Midway leading up to the main circus tent, while the Sideshow performers' trailers are parked in an adjoining section of the lot, a neighborhood within a neighborhood on the circus grounds. Few others traveling with the circus actually have much contact with those, shall we say, "different" types of people. You knew they were there, the same way that upper class people are aware of the existence of society's fringe dwellers. But you didn't see them very often.

Several years before my tenure, our circus's Sideshow had a fat man who tipped the scales at well over six hundred pounds. No one who paid a separate admission to the Sideshow and who came face to face with the Fat Man felt cheated. Our fat man was a bona fide extra, extra, extra large individual, and he exceeded the expectations of pretty much all of our circus goers.

He didn't do any tricks other than to eat enormous quantities of food. His family traveled with him, and his wife spent a great deal of time each day going to the grocery store in whatever location we found ourselves, to buy him the tools of his trade . . . namely, food.

No one exactly remembers how the trouble began with the Fat Man. Some people think that the Fat Man's wife saw something about the dangers of being overweight on *60 Minutes* or *48 Hours*. Other people think that someone left a copy of a Dr. Atkins weight loss book leaning against their circus trailer. Some people think that it might have been the Fat Man's idea himself, that he was simply tired of being so heavy in a society that placed so much emphasis on appearance.

No matter. One way or another, the Fat Man's wife started to buy him healthier food. Fruit instead of Fruit Loops. Onion rings instead of Ring

Dings. Rice cakes instead of chocolate cakes. Rumor had it that the Fat Man had become . . . a vegetarian . . . although I could never uncover any proof for this assertion.

When you weigh six hundred pounds, you can drop fifty or seventy-five pounds and nobody will notice a thing. It took four or five months of modified eating before the Fat Man's weight loss became noticeable to anyone in the circus. Since the management of the circus had little to do with the Sideshow on a day-to-day basis, the Fat Man managed to shed a third of his girth, two hundred pounds, before management became concerned.

A four hundred pound fat man is still an intriguing Sideshow attraction. But a four hundred-pounder really doesn't have the awe of a man who weighs six hundred pounds. As legend has it, the circus powers-that-be informed the Fat Man, "Start eating again or you're fired. We can't charge money for people to look at a relatively thin fat man."

The Fat Man understood that his job was on the line, but he liked the way he was looking in the mirror, the real mirror that is, not a freaky Sideshow mirror. For a guy who could barely bestir himself to get out of his chair during the day except to meet the most basic of nature's calls, the Fat Man, slightly more svelte each month, could now be seen taking walks, admittedly brief walks, around the perimeter of the circus neighborhood each morning.

The Fat Man was getting in shape.

Circus administrators came to the Fat Man a second time and explained that his unorthodox approach to eating, at least unorthodox by typical Sideshow fat man standards, simply could not be tolerated. He had to quit exercising, go back to eating in an unhealthy manner, and pack on a few more lbs, or his job would be the next thing lost.

The Fat Man listened carefully to what his employers had to say, but he continued his low calorie ways.

Before long, he was down to three hundred and fifty pounds.

His wife bought him his first pair of running shoes.

The Fat Man was now down to the size of a respectable NFL lineman—big, but not plump enough for a Sideshow.

The inevitable finally occurred. The Fat Man . . . was fired.

Some people suggested to the Fat Man that he get a lawyer and fight it. But the Fat Man, increasingly becoming the Large if Somewhat Portly Yet Debonair Man, wouldn't think of it. He understood that the terms of his employment required him to be grossly overweight. And neither he nor his wife wanted him to live like that any longer. He recognized that it was time to move on.

The Fat Man used his severance pay to buy a whole new wardrobe. He had broken below the three hundred pound barrier the last time anyone at the circus heard anything about him. For all we know, he now weighs a hundred and eighty pounds and does triathlons.

It was a strange paradox that the main show performers, including the trapeze artists, animal trainers, jugglers, and tight rope walkers, had to stay trim and physically fit in order to keep their jobs, while the Sideshow performers couldn't keep their jobs if they did the same thing. Aberration was the key to employment with the Sideshow.

The lesson of the Fat Man is clear. From the circus's point of view, his diminishing weight meant diminishing returns for the circus. People want to see a really, really fat, fat man in a Sideshow, not a guy who looks like he could run a marathon if he would just knock off the Ben & Jerry's.

Performance Tool: Crisis Avoidance

On the surface, the story about the circus Fat Man losing weight is just pure hilarity. The determination of the girth appropriate to keep his job was initially undefined, but became obvious as the weight loss continued. His diminishing size meant diminishing effect on the audience. Being fat was his act.

The time came in the career of the Fat Man when he wanted to evolve and move into other careers. With the help of his wife, he slowly made changes that allowed him to seek other forms of employment. He realized that remaining grossly obese wasn't the smartest way of conducting his life and earning a living. We all come to awareness in our lives that change our priorities and consequently our goals and objectives. Self-motivated change is easier to deal with than change forced on us.

The Fat Man's job in the circus was secure as long as he remained extremely fat. But job security isn't always the best circumstance if security negatively affects our health and welfare. There are those critical times when we need to change because we need it for the betterment of our lives and the lives of those who depend on us. It's these times when we have to face the fear of the unknown and deal with change. If we don't, we can face crisis.

The need to lose weight is an obvious need. It's visual, and therefore not refutable. But what do we do when we can't overtly see the need for change? Feelings of disconnect in our work can slowly creep up on us. There doesn't have to be anyone to blame; there's no visible cause. But yet, we find we're not happy and not growing. We're just grazing on work, solely earning money. This is the most difficult and crucial time to make changes because it requires a great deal of selfevaluation, planning, and courage. We are taking big chances when we choose to redirect our work. We are leaving a familiar group of people, a secure environment, and a steady income. Initiating career change when things look good on the face of our current job or career puts us in the spotlight among our peers, our friends, and our families—all people whom we want to respect us.

Conversely, when change is forced upon us it seems that we have less to lose in regard to people's expectations of us, and most importantly of our own expectations of ourselves. We are kinder to ourselves if at first we don't succeed in a new job because we were forced to change.

It is absolutely imperative, at times, to make changes in our careers if we want to be happy and fulfilled with our work. We will receive diminishing returns in terms of the way we use our time, our skills, and our talents if we don't make changes when our hearts are not in our work. Fat chance of enjoying our lives any other way!

Negotiating With Horse Sense

One of the great things about traveling for business is that you get to spend a lot of time reading—on planes, in hotel rooms, while dining alone. I love to read, so that aspect of the job worked out perfectly for me. I got a chance to read business books and keep up with what other people were thinking and saying about the business world.

I had just finished reading Herb Cohen's book *You Can Negotiate Anything* when I arrived in Savannah, Georgia for my next marketing assignment. I was fascinated with the basic concept that Cohen proffered in the book: everything on earth can be negotiated, even things with fixed price tags. Cohen writes that just because a figure is written down on a price tag, whether we are talking about a refrigerator in an appliance store or advertising time on a rate card, it still can be negotiated. He offered examples of products that are widely accepted as negotiable, like cars and homes. Then he went on to list other products that are never considered to be negotiable items, like clothing that has not yet gone on sale.

I was keenly interested in the subject of negotiating because I did a great deal of negotiating on behalf of the circus. Whenever I saw advertising rate cards from radio and TV stations, or newspapers, I would always ask if they could come down on the prices. And usually they did. I would also negotiate promotions with area businesses, and one of the greatest incentives that I could offer was complimentary tickets to the circus. Everybody loves free tickets, and those free tickets drove down the cost of promoting the circus.

One evening in Savannah, after a hard day of selling Junior Clown Academy makeup classes and animated animal act promotions to the media for sponsorship, I went to the Savannah Mall for a relaxing night of shopping. It was also in my mind to put Herb Cohen's strategy to the test, that you can negotiate even so called fixed prices.

I found a stunning solid gold ring at a jewelry store, and I wanted it badly. After trying it on and seeing that it was a perfect fit and a gorgeous design for my hand, I nonetheless departed the store without purchasing it. I felt it was overpriced and out of my budget. Returning to my hotel that evening, I reviewed Cohen's philosophy and decided to devise a plan to buy that ring. I identified the price I wanted to pay for the ring, along with support logic as to why the store should mark the ring down to my price: it was too small a size for most women to wear; and if someone *could* wear it it would take a long finger to make the ring look appropriate for the hand. The ring was much like Cinderella's slipper.

The next day, I planned to go back to the store and lobby my case with the manager. All day long, I could barely focus on my work because I was so excited about my upcoming negotiating session at the mall. That evening, I went to the jewelry store and found that the ring had been marked down to a price that was *below* what I was going to offer! Incredulous, I bought the ring and left without any further discussion. I was thrilled to get the ring, but I was extremely disappointed that I didn't get to use my arguments and Herb's theory.

So I immediately went to an upscale clothing store in the same mall in order to convert my ring negotiating logic into clothing negotiating logic. It was time to put into effect another one of Herb's strategies, this one relating to time. Herb Cohen suggests that the amount of time that the customer takes with the salesperson in discussing a sale is parallel to the amount of the discount the salesperson will give in order to close the sale. In other words, time truly is money, and the more time a salesperson has invested in a particular sale, the more anxious he or she will be to make that sale, and the better the discount to which you can look forward. In other words, salespeople trade their time for the customer's money. I have to admit that I took a lot of this salesclerk's time.

Finally, it was show time. I chose the item of apparel I wanted, and then I identified in my mind the price I was willing to pay for it. The salesclerk, of course, said that the clothing wasn't negotiable. I had to wait until it was on sale if I wanted to pay less then the ticket price for it. It was time to go to work. I explained that I was only there on business for a short time, promoting the circus (Everybody loves the circus!) and I didn't have time to wait for the sale. I had money now that I wanted to spend with that salesclerk. All I was asking for was the sale price . . . right now.

I'm here to tell you that it worked! Herb was right! They reduced the dress to just about the price that I wanted to spend. I agreed to what they offered, and I went home happy.

Performance Tool: Mental Chess

Mental Chess helped me get a reduced price for a dress that wasn't on sale and that had no flaws. You might wonder what buying a dress in a Savannah, Georgia shopping mall might have to do with your career. Answer: plenty. I successfully used the negotiating techniques described in this story in many subsequent jobs, such as negotiating a salary with a teddy bear company (described in next section in "Performance Tips") and, after my circus career by convincing the Northern Trust Bank in Sarasota, Florida that they should give me a loan to start a Mary Kay distributorship, with absolutely no hard assets with which to collateralize the loan. Herb Cohen's strategy in *You Can Negotiate Anything* is indeed an extremely good model for developing negotiating skills.

Let's take a look at how these Mental Chess strategies play out in the job market. People generally take jobs with the salary and terms they are initially offered. Why do people do this? Perhaps they are afraid that if they turn the offer down, they will lose the job. But this is rarely if ever the case if the employer likes you and sees value in your skills and work experience! Ask any employer, and he or she will tell you that one of the hardest parts of growing a business is finding the right people—talented, competent individuals with integrity—to fill positions. And yet, at least in the initial negotiation phase, most employers are likely to offer salaries and benefits at the low end of what they would consider acceptable. Most people leap at those offers, without realizing that they could hold out for a better salary and better terms. By communicating our needs and our desires with the logic to support them, we extend the negotiating portion of the job or performance interview. When we do this we have a fighting chance of increasing the compensation package. We involve the employer's time and thought process. We engage their emotion and their logic. We can redress the offer. Truly, just about everything can be negotiated.

Why should anything be non-negotiable? The legal term for one party having all the bargaining power is "adhesion." The word calls to mind the adjective adhesive, as in adhesive tape. The implication is that one side has the power and the other side is truly stuck. My philosophy of creating equally balanced relationships means that neither side should have all the power, and neither should be stuck. This is just as true when you are selling a product to a customer as when you are selling your own services to a potential employer. You are most likely entitled to more than what the employer is offering, but you'll only feel that way if you recognize the power, and commercial value, you have in any given negotiation. Most people feel so passive and powerless when they go into negotiations that they leap at the first offer. It's time to quit doing that.

My philosophy of creating equally balanced relationships factors into all of my business deals. Sometimes I'm stronger than at other times in the negotiating process. But Herb Cohen is absolutely right: nobody has more power than the other person. Winners and losers are determined by the way people feel about their own level of power. I do believe that anything can be negotiated. I also believe that honoring the person with whom you are negotiating, and not trying to destroy that person or grind him or her into the ground on price, adds to the success of the negotiations and the relationship. It does make for a perfect game of Mental Chess.

When you are in a negotiating situation, whether you are buying an article of clothing or negotiating for your next job, use the Mental Chess strategy by asking yourself these questions: What's it worth to me? What can I afford to accept? What can't I afford to accept? What exactly is my source of power? Where is my power in the negotiation? What is it that I have that this employer or client cannot do without? Chances are, you really do have much more power and negotiable value in any given relationship than you realize.

The issue then becomes that of recognizing that you have a right to exercise the option of negotiation. In Mental Chess you negotiate with yourself before you engage in successful negotiation for the advancement of a business opportunity. This is where you decide what your time is worth, what your contributions are worth, and how you think you should be compensated for what you bring to the table. That's the aspect of Mental Chess that takes place between you and you.

When I was negotiating with the salesclerk for a reduced price on a dress in the Savannah Mall, I made a strong case as to why I deserved a lower price for that garment. I didn't beg, cajole, browbeat, or argue. I simply set forth a logical explanation for why the sales clerk should lower the price. And the logic in fact made sense to her. Most people think that successful negotiators rely on emotional tactics like bullying, triggering guilt, or otherwise attempting to manipulate others in a demeaning way. You don't have to do any of that when you employ Mental Chess. All you have to do is give the other side a logical way to see the value in your point of view, and you'll soon see objections come tumbling down.

Ring Two: Performance Tips

Now that we've seen how the Performance Tools played out at the circus, let's go deeper. This section gives some helpful hints through Performance Tips to help claim the power and control we want in the work place, and lay claim to that which is rightfully ours to have. The premise behind the Performance Tips is this: *you can create, choose, and change the way you express power and control in your business relationships.*

You have the power to create much needed balance with employers, clients, and coworkers, and eliminate the fear that we attach to people we perceive as more powerful than us. You have the right to be respected, even in the most entry-level positions. You have the ability to change your image within your company, but only if you know how to effectively communicate and behave. You can be a stronger person if you understand the techniques and practices available to use.

This next concept is the key to understanding and believing in your power: *every relationship is a buyer/seller relationship.* We are either employers and clients, or employees and vendor/consultants. These are, at their very essence, buyer/ seller relationships. Employers and clients buy the services and products of employees and vendor/consultants. Buyers need sellers; employers need employees. The reverse is also true. Buyers, those with money as their negotiable power, are perceived to have greater power than sellers, those with goods or services as their negotiable power. Buyers do not have more power than sellers. Equal power exists in proportion to the terms of the relationship. Money buys goods and services, but it doesn't buy the purveyor; it doesn't buy you, if you are the seller. You can ultimately mitigate the power that may be holding you back in your dealings with your employers and clients through this understanding.

There's a caveat in the buyer/seller relationship that universally levels the playing field: we are all vendors to someone. We are either selling our time, our knowledge, our experiences, our goods, our services, or some combination thereof, to someone else. We are all sellers and vendors accountable to other people. At the highest level of corporate authority, CEOs of publicly traded companies are selling their expertise to their stockholders. The annual stockholder's meeting is the accountability meeting for CEOs. Ultimately, for the wealthiest people and companies in the world, there's accountability to the U.S. government for taxes and for growing monopolies, the things that bring down the biggest and the best of industry's leaders.

Well-respected, high-achieving people, make tough choices under tough conditions. The choices we make determine our fate. Difficult choices build strength of character. Difficult choices allow us to craft and retool our careers, and develop business relationships with more power and with more control.

In order to really feel a sense of power in business relationships, focus on your negotiable value to the buyer. We always need to recognize and define that value. There is a very specific reason why a client or an employer hires you. Know that reason, embrace that reason, enhance that reason, and use it when it's time to negotiate with your buyer.

We need to understand that work is the exchange of goods and services for money. That's it. Pretty simple. There are lots of buyers, and there are lots of opportunities that represent career advancement. You can only take advantage of those opportunities if you can hold your own, and act with power, in those relationships. The most important part of achieving success with the buyer/seller concept: choose the right work and environment for your talents, skills, and lifestyle preference. When the buyer and the seller are a perfect match, the power flows evenly between them.

You can negotiate for almost anything you want if you understand the needs of the buyer, if you can fulfill those needs, and if you can define and support the amount of compensation you want for the work effort it will take, and the skills required for fulfilling those needs.

I felt powerful as a person when I was with the circus. I felt validated with my choice to join the circus. I made the right career choice for my lifestyle needs and for my skill set. I was fulfilling the goal I set for myself in college, which, oddly enough, started with lifestyle considerations in my work. All of my talents and interests, to include writing, public speaking, business management, contract negotiating, promotion, marketing, sales, and entertainment, were all showcased by the circus job. And the lifestyle suited me perfectly. I loved living in hotels, traveling to remote places, and learning about the topography of our country. I was making enough money to live a gypsy's life well. The routine felt great, which allowed me to feel powerful. To know that I finally found the right job that supported my chosen lifestyle was invigorating.

When choosing a career, or interviewing for a great job, never ever think you have *nothing* special to offer! Everyone has something special, if just simply their personalities. Sometimes, a good personality actually ranks higher than experience or skills with many buyers. I remember an illustration of this from my time at the circus. There were eight of us in the marketing department. We worked in sequential rotation of the tour dates for the season. There was only one advance promoter, though. The difference between the marketing directors and the advance promoter was that this singular person would go into *every* town about three months ahead of the show. The advance promoter would only book the biggest media promotions and establish media partnerships that required a much longer advance time than the standard two to three weeks that the marketing directors were given for their campaigns.

Daryl Wallace, one of the eight marketing directors, was a young Clark Gable and Cary Grant rolled up into one spectacular looking human being. His personality was pleasant; he was wonderful to be around and so people just naturally gravitated towards him. He was good at his job as marketing director, but so were the other seven people in our department. Out of all the excellent choices the circus could have made, Daryl was chosen to be the next advance promoter. Why? He was the most social of the eight marketing directors to be around. There was a lot of socializing connected to the advance promoter job. Daryl presented one more reason, by way of his gift of cocktail gab, to qualify him for the promotion. So there's no such thing as "nothing special." Even when skills, salaries, work experience, or other terms are equal, there is always a way to differentiate us from the pack.

I'd like to share with you now a troupe of Performance Tips for creating better business relationships, thus preventing your career from turning into a cacophony of bad acts and judgment calls. After all, a real circus is terrific if you want a day off to go see the lions and tigers, the acrobats, and the clowns. But there shouldn't be anything circus-like about your work life! Here's how to keep your business relationships from turning into an unwieldy three-ring circus.

You Have Marketable Value

Everyone has a market value to trade with his or her clients and employers. Your market value is determined by the evaluation of your relevance to the needs of your employer or client; by your perceived value within your industry; and then by your ranking within the needs of society. Market value carries with it marketable power. You have power commensurate with the breadth of your business relationships.

Marketable value is the tension that balances relationships. This concept is at the crux of every healthy business relationship. Knowing that you have market value in any business relationship, and therefore marketable power, can set the tone and pave the way for security and advancement with your employers and clients. Jimmy Buffet wrote a song years ago called "It's My Job." It says everyone's job has value, even a street cleaner's. Jimmy further says that we can either do a job well, or poorly. It's up to us to place a value on our services, and we do this by the quality of the work we provide. No job is too insignificant that it can't make a difference if done well. Any job done well continues to add to the value, and consequently to the power of the seller of those services.

Knowing you have market power is key to using it. Given that you are excellent at your work, and have self-confidence (absolutely necessary) about your work effort, you can maintain a balance of respect and power in your business relationships. The burden of proof for power is on the seller. The seller will be the one who initially tips the scales of power and respect.

An equally balanced relationship, though, doesn't preclude the need for a leader. There is always a leader, a person who puts finality on work related decisions. That person is typically the employer or client. Sometimes the seller has more decision-making responsibilities. But there has to be *a* person who has ultimate decision-making responsibilities. It has to be someone's role to put closure on issues. That still doesn't give the leader more power. The seller can choose to leave the buyer at any point, unless contractually obligated to a specific finish date.

Here's a wild example of an equally balanced relationship: Dave Hoover, the lion trainer with the Clyde Beatty-Cole Bros. Circus, and his animals. Dave explained his philosophy to me regarding his relationships with his lions and tigers, his "cats." Dave said he felt he had "as much power over the cats as the cats had over him." The cats are the sellers, with their extraordinary physical strength as their negotiable commodity. Dave is the buyer with extraordinary mental strength as his value. Lions and tigers have a three second attention span, longer than many people! This brief attention span allowed Dave to change his movements and his props every three seconds in order to stay alive and prevent the cats from mauling him. The balance of power in this relationship is mental versus physical.

To the audience though, the seeming imbalance between the physical strength of the cats over Dave created fear as the negotiable commodity that the cat act sold to the audience, the *real* buyers in the larger relationship. As I mentioned earlier, we are all vendors to someone.

Remember, the tension in the relationship comes from the sellers. In this example, the lions and tigers are the sellers. The lions' and tigers' strength and killing capacity is the marketable power that served as the tension that balanced their relationship with Dave. The fear of Dave getting mauled made that working relationship profitable to the circus, and to Dave and his beasts. People go to the circus for death-defying acts. The cats provided the impetus for the act, which then became a marketable commodity for the circus.

Dave's marketable value to the lions and tigers was as the provider of food, housing, and safety from exotics poachers. Any pet owner knows that their animals recognize the value in their owners' services. If the food keeps coming, and a shelter is available, pets will generally continue to provide their marketable value of comfort and protection. As long as Dave kept providing food, shelter, and care, the animals continued to provide tricks for performances so that Dave could earn a living and the circus could have a wild animal act for the audience.

One of the most famous lion trainers of all time, Clyde Beatty, a previous owner of the circus that bears his name, was renowned for putting his head in a lion's mouth. Lots of respect and balance there, eh? Don't you feel like you're putting your head in a lion's mouth when you have to deal with disrespectful employers and clients—people who try to tip the balance of power in their direction constantly? Don't allow the beheading of your respect and power.

In the circus story "Win Emotional Juggling Matches," I explained my response when the circus didn't pay my salary on time. I didn't threaten to quit. I didn't want to quit. I negotiated for a brief vacation until my paycheck arrived. What gave me the courage to do this? I recognized that I had as much value and power in the relationship as my employer. I needed a paycheck, while they needed me to do my job as marketing director. If the circus wasn't going to fulfill this part of their contractual obligation to me, I did not feel obligated to give them what I had promised, a dedicated, uninterrupted work effort. Three days after my negotiated vacation had begun, my paycheck arrived, and I went back to work.

If you develop an understanding of your marketable value and power, I believe you will enjoy more balanced relationships.

Self-Respect Breeds Power

One way to appear powerful is through the engagement of respect. There are three categories of respect: self-respect, earned respect, and shared respect. We all want to receive respect in our work places. We want the respect of our coworkers. But we especially want the respect of our employers and clients. Too often in the business world, we must request respect. Some people give respect naturally. Others, either as a function of their personalities or as a business tactic, begin their business relationships by exercising disrespect.

It's said that if we want respect, we have to do two things: give respect and earn respect. That's true. Sometimes we have to demand it, given that we have earned it, and clearly express how we want to get it. Simply asking for respect forces people to look at us differently, because it shows we respect ourselves. Requiring respect shows that we have eliminated the fear that can come with buyer/seller relationships. Bottom line, if we show that we respect ourselves, we will get more respect from others.

Some people mistake kindness for weakness. Some people misconstrue politeness for weakness. It's vital to set your standards for respect at the beginning of each relationship. Bubbles the Clown, in "Don't Take Orders From Clowns," thought nothing of ordering me to bail him out of the police skirmish at the Muscle Shoals Mall in Alabama. He wasn't interested in approaching me in such a way that allowed my dignity and authority to remain intact. Bubbles was only interested in *his* goals, and in *his* needs. The way he talked to me was rude, disrespectful, and inappropriate for my position and level of responsibility. Artistic relationships are some of the most fragile business relationships because of the uniqueness of the artist's skills, and the singular nature of their role. It's hard for a show to go on without the talent available for the show. When artistic temperaments flare right before a show or a media interview, artists tend to get their way unless they have strong business managers around to help put disagreements in perspective.

If I wanted to act with self-respect in the Muscle Shoals Mall parking lot, and maintain control over this volatile relationship with our premier clown, I had to play hardball. So I did—in a measured way. I did check out the jail cell before allowing Bubbles to go behind bars for the evening. I saw to his need for nourishment by reviewing the take-out menu at the sheriff's desk. I even took his dog, Kitty, back with me to my hotel. I did take a chance with the reaction of the home office in exercising power with my chosen method for maintaining control . . . jail time for Bubbles. Fortunately, I remained employed, and was even complimented by my careful and thoughtful resourcefulness. I think my earned respect level rose with the home office.

"Win Emotional Juggling Matches," the story about my paycheck being held hostage until the circus made more money, served as a catalyst for redefining my self-respect and for rebalancing power in regard to unilateral contractual changes. There was no deadline given for the paycheck hiatus, or discussion with me prior to the decision. Possibly I would have worked out terms to a request for a different payment schedule if my needs had been taken into consideration. But since the decision wasn't mutual I felt I would be acquiescing power if I let that incident slip by. I didn't quit. I didn't get angry. I calmly explained how I felt and what I needed and expected in the relationship. Plus, I kept in touch with the home office each day I was vacationing in Dallas so that they felt some degree of security.

I think we are aggrieved on a daily basis with random abuses to basic respect from everyone around us. If we cultivate self-respect and the power that goes with it, we can always set our boundaries and parameters for respectful behavior from others.

Power Beats Cower

To successfully exercise power, act like you have nothing to lose. This is a concept you'll find in politics, sports, and entertainment—three of the most competitive work environments in our society. Acting like you have nothing to lose is the mental outlook necessary for winning. In order to perform in front of thousands, if not millions of people, ball players, politicians, and performers all share one thing in common: they have to put their fear of losing, of non-acceptance, of public disapproval, of failing aside, and go to work each day in front of huge numbers of spectators. How are they able to do this? They have to focus on their goals—winning a game, hitting a high note, or delivering a compelling speech.

So it is with you, too. You have to risk losing a client or a job, at times, to reach a greater goal—self-expression. You may need to support a philosophical or ethical position, to make a necessary change in your department, or to rebalance a relationship. Yet sometimes losing a job or a client is the best and only way to go. Losing work can make us richer in the long run, allowing us to find something else we like better. There are countless stories of people reaching their highest levels of success because they turned a job loss into a window of opportunity and started another career.

Consider role-playing a past experience that required you to stand your ground in a disagreement with an employer, a client, or a management superior. Did you say what you wanted to say? Would you respond differently in hindsight? Was money an issue? Did you fear losing the job or the client because you weren't financially stable? How freeing is the idea of making decisions based purely on your belief system? We have to choose our battles while we fight to uphold our values.

Part of exercising power means exercising our right to choose and our right to refuse. At times we have to choose to walk away. When we choose to lose, we start to exercise control over our careers and function with more power over right decision-making.

To use a circus metaphor, you are certainly walking a tight rope each time you try to redefine a relationship. Yet most of the time, you'll get some degree of what you want. Make sure your request is fair, both to you and to your buyer. If you do strike out because of an irresolvable issue with your buyer, it will most certainly be for the betterment of your career.

Several of the circus stories in Ring One had a point where I risked losing my job, and risked fulfilling performance commitments, because I had to take a stand and make an unpopular or unconventional decision: "Clowning Around With Crisis," "Don't Take Orders From Clowns," and "Win Emotional Juggling Matches." My dealings with Bubbles the Clown in Panama City, Florida and Muscle Shoals, Alabama were defining moments in my relationship with him as well as with circus management. It showed that I was willing to take calculated risks to maintain control over spontaneous, out-of-control events. Those decisions showed that I understood how to use the power of my position.

"Win Emotional Juggling Matches" (aka 'paycheck held hostage') showed I had the courage of my convictions in regard to the seriousness of maintaining an equally balanced relationship with my employer. How would you have handled that situation? Has an employer or a client ever changed the payment terms of your relationship without consulting you first?

Within my role as marketing director for the circus, I had to make advertising decisions with media outlets all the time. Sometimes the deals they offered just weren't good enough. And sometimes we were in towns so small that there were very few choices available for advertising and promotion. Still, I had to seek alternate forms of extended advertising and marketing if I couldn't make the right deals for the advertising campaign. I had to have the confidence that my saying "no" would lead to a creative and thus more productive outcome. And it did. In 1987 I was awarded Marketing Director of the Year. That year I veered from the typical blueprint we all used for media campaigns and developed alternate strategies for marketing the circus. Those alternate choices served to take traditionally revenue-losing cities and turned them into profit-making bookings for the circus. I would like to add that I had the circus management's support to make changes based on my past record of achievement and the strength of the relationship the circus and I had cultivated.

There's power in taking responsibility for tough decision-making. Power breeds strength. People respect strength. Don't cower; exercise the power of decision—making.

Communication Is Nectar for Power

For circus performers the rigging has to be set firmly, positioned correctly, and used authoritatively in order to have tragedy-free performances. In business, words are the rigging with which we make our work performance great and tragedy—free.

There is an art to communication, much like an acrobatic display of athletic prowess. The words we choose, and the way we position our language will affect the outcome of a conversation, a negotiation, or a debate. Executing responsible communication with timing and precision is an art.

It's a delicate and difficult task to communicate with people who are confrontational, or a threat to our security. These situations are manifested in a variety of ways from disagreements over money, contractual arguments, job advancement, or my favorite communication challenge, responding to the dreaded legal letter. In any case, you have more power and control than you may realize in achieving specific goals, influencing people's behavior, and resolving a disagreement, just by the way you craft your language. There are two steps to artful communication in a contentious situation. *First,* organize your thoughts and carefully identify the goals you want to achieve. Here's your checklist: review any printed documents that have preceded the problem; use logic and objectivity in your analysis; try not to be accusatory when organizing your defense; identify your opponent's moral center and address it in your support strategy; and, own responsibility, for you may be culpable, too. Keep your responses as short and simple as possible; eliminate extraneous information.

Second, develop your communication strategy. Think through language options to communicate your position and achieve your goal in a direct yet respectful way. Never use the second person pronoun "you" when crafting your argument. Always use third person pronouns "they, it, them," or first person plural "we." The word "you" has an accusatory ring to it and puts people on the defensive. When people are on the defensive they try to protect themselves by fighting to be right rather than accommodating a settlement. Third person "they" and first person "we" plural pronouns help take the heat off your opponent because they establish a team effort approach towards discussing and resolving an issue. People are likely to be more open to discussion if they don't feel isolated and threatened. The best results would be to have your opponent concede and still work with you. We're not out for blood and bad feelings, just results.

I want to emphasize this one important point again: *choose your words and position your argument so that it is a collaborative, problem-solving exercise between both parties.* The goal in artful communication is to avoid feelings of guilt that your opponent could have. It's deadly when guilt emerges as the dominant emotion, because the natural reaction of someone who feels guilty is to fight. If you address the core moral center of your opponent, and appeal to his or her sense of right and duty, you have a much better chance of reaching an equitable solution.

Ask a friend to role-play an argument and serve as your devil's advocate, before you go to babble battle. Your friend may have responses that you didn't foresee. Role-playing may identify responsibilities that you need to own in order to have a reasonable discussion. In justifying your position, and in dealing with the fear or anger that confrontation brings, you just may be overlooking your own culpability. In artful communication we need to be honest about our responsibility, too. Ironically, when we admit responsibility, we strengthen our position. We don't lose power but gain back control and respect through responsible, careful, honest communication.

In "Avoid Pratt Falls" I had to take responsibility and pay Johnny Pugh for the fine the Children's Theater Company received at the Halloween Show from the Naples, Florida Police. I had to admit my failure to properly evaluate the area in which we were located. I owned the responsibility for police involvement, and showed Johnny that I did care about keeping our relationship respectful and balanced. When I then offered a workable solution to enable us to complete the second half of the show in Boca Raton (my big goal), I was in a better position to lobby and negotiate.

We've all heard the saying "you can catch more flies with honey than vinegar." It's absolutely true in the business world. Artful communication will allow for successful outcomes to power thwarting problems.

Contracts Control Power

Put everything in writing. Create a paper trail. Keep a printed file of all e-mail communications. Never rely on verbal contracts for projects of any significance. This practice will allow you to control your revenue, your work, your reputation, and your relationships. Without written documentation you have nothing with which to support your position if disagreements occur with your employer, client, or co-worker. Memory isn't accurate. Printed words don't lie. The person in a dispute who keeps all documentation has control.

Contracts are extremely important documents. Contracts are a point of reference and are vital to every business relationship. Contracts are not for the purpose of making people honest. Instead, the purpose of a contract is to help honest people remember the terms of the agreement exactly.

The main reason written contracts are vital is more for the sake of memory. Indeed, lawyers talk about "memorializing" terms in an agreement. We are all way too busy to remember every detail of a business deal months after the deal is struck, whether it is an employment arrangement, or the sale of a product or service. Memory sometimes changes with the passage of time. Memory is not a solid reference point for an agreement. Only written contracts serve that purpose. Clarification of deal points is needed at times. Normal, innocent questions frequently arise about obligations, responsibilities and execution.

Many things will need to be redefined over the course of a contractual relationship. If a contract is in place, the task of reviewing terms is easier. If no written contract exists, there is no objective reference point upon which both parties can rely.

Never underestimate the power of the written word. Two parties might have a different memory of price, of delivery date, of start time for a performance, or a myriad of other debatable issues. By documenting the key facts of a deal in writing, both sides have something to which they can refer, thus avoiding many potential disputes and moments of bad feelings.

When the circus started giving commissions to marketing directors, based on ticket sales per show date, I asked them to put the formula in writing. We didn't work with employment contracts for the marketing team at that time; only performers had contracts. I was asking the circus to redefine a part of our relationship by documenting a financial arrangement. Thank heavens we did have a contract in place for the newly installed commission incentive, because the circus and I had a different memory regarding commissions on a couple of my towns with large enough ticket sales. Without a written contract in place, we would not have settled on a figure acceptable to both sides as easily and quickly as we did.

There's a famous story about the singer formerly, or perhaps currently, known as Prince. News stories reported that at one point he was renegotiating with his record label, and he became highly incensed when they would not agree to either let him change the style of his music or cancel his contract. His ultimate attitude and position then reportedly became an issue of trust and contract relevance. He purportedly responded that if his record company didn't trust him enough to make a deal on the basis of a handshake, and allow Prince to function as he solely chose, then he should not remain in business with them. Prince wanted to change the style of his music for future albums, and his record company wanted him to keep working in the style in which his audience was familiar, so that the record company could count on future album sales. Artists typically have these disagreements at various points in their careers with their record companies. Prince then supposedly asked to be released from his contract. His record company wouldn't agree. That's when Prince decided that if he had to comply with the contract for the duration of the defined time, he would act like the slave he felt he was, and tattooed that symbol on his face that he said represented his slavery to the record company.

He stopped using his name Prince and asked to be referred to as the slave symbol only. He then started ranting about the ugliness of contracts, that contracts made people dishonest, and that he would never enter into a written contract again because he contended that contracts ruined business relationships. Prince further contended that if people were honest, they wouldn't need contracts.

I disagree. My position is that contracts are meant to reference and define a relationship, especially intricate business deals that people can't possibly commit to memory. Record contracts are riddled with complicated stuff like percentage splits, payment dates, distribution networks, music content—just a lot of detail that can be remembered differently as time goes by.

Prince, in my opinion, acted in a one-sided, temperamental way. I contend that Prince couldn't be trusted to uphold the dignity and terms of the contract he signed, although I understand the need for an artist to be able to make changes with his art. I think that Prince had two other options: he could have negotiated to cover any loss of profit that a new style of music may have engendered; or he could have paid his record company future projected earnings in order to be released from the contract. If he had taken either of these options, the record company could have gotten what they wanted, which was profit for the money already invested in Prince's career; and Prince could have moved on with making his music his way. This proposed theoretical decision could have put Prince in a respectable position of responsibility, and maybe given him a fighting chance to make changes from the original contract.

The contentious artist formerly, or currently, known as Prince is a terrific singer, dancer, composer, and overall musical genius. I think where Prince missed the boat was with regard to the purpose of a written contract. A written contract is not about creating trust between two parties. Either trust is there or it doesn't exist. A written agreement serves to help two parties who already trust each other to avoid disputes by putting down on paper, for both of them to see and to sign, exactly what they are agreeing to do. Without a contract, your lawyers are likely to party like it's 1999.

I learned this lesson in contractual awareness the hard way as a performer, in Cape Cod, Massachusetts when I was the elephant ride ticket seller. It was a rainy, cold day in May; the first time that season that we had experienced such inclement conditions. Although I had never reviewed circus policy regarding their expectations of me if rain or bad weather ensued, I assumed I had the day off. After all, I had to stand outside on the Midway to perform this job. If I stood in the rain, I might catch a cold, and then I would not be able to fulfill my duties as the Dancing Bear.

Or so I thought.

The Midway opened one hour before the afternoon show, at 3:30pm. About 3:45pm, Chris Rawls, the circus manager, banged on my trailer door asking why I wasn't in my booth next to the elephant ride. Children and the elephant were waiting for me to open. I was shocked! I popped my head outside to confirm that I wasn't dreaming. It certainly was rainy, windy and freezing cold—conditions that may be no surprise to residents of Cape Cod, but certainly news to me. Something still didn't register. "You mean," I asked, "you want me to be uncomfortable while I work? I could get sick if I stand outside today."

You see, I had never asked about the work conditions. I had never found out whether they would be influenced by the weather. And yes, it turned out that the circus expected me to be in my post every single day, regardless of the weather. Management did go to the novelty toy stand for a clown umbrella to put in my booth for protection. But I was out there, in the wind and the rain, selling tickets and watching people riding that elephant. You'd have thought that I worked for the postal service!

If I had taken the time to at least discuss the policies about working outside in bad weather, I wouldn't have had to be dragged from my trailer. I would have been at my post, bundled up and ready to go. So I learned that one the hard way. I apparently didn't pay attention to some working conditions while I was in the marketing department.

I always recommend that sellers write the contracts. I think it's good for the seller to put the language in his or her own tone of voice with his or her own set of parameters and guidelines. This will give you the control to define terms a little more to your liking. By writing the contracts you have also set the tone for the nature of your relationship. This shows seriousness of purpose, self-respect, and business acumen. Employers may have standard contracts prepared for employees, but there's no reason why the employee can't come in with his or her contract, too. The buyer may give you a bit of resistance because you have the temerity to be so efficient and thorough, but you'll sure be given respect.

In a client/vendor relationship, the seller most often writes the contracts. Don't expect a contract to turn a dishonest person into an honest one. That's not what contracts do. If either party in a negotiation isn't honest, getting signatures on a contract will do nothing to prevent dishonesty. That person will hire battalions of lawyers to deny the validity of the written terms of your agreement. In regards to honesty, the purpose of a contract is to keep honest people from getting slaughtered by dishonest people.

Have a respect for contracts. Carefully read and choose every word in a contract. Anticipate worst-case scenarios while negotiating contracts, because unforeseen circumstances do happen as time goes on. Emotions enter the picture when memory fails us and they take their toll on the outcome. And, people can see things differently after the work begins. Things just don't go as planned sometimes. Contracts will be your safety nets and can prevent a freefall if unexpected issues arise.

Control Your PDR

Everybody has a point of diminishing returns (PDR). That's the point where your job or a project is no longer worth your continued time and effort. Several things have to be considered in order to determine where that diminishing return point is: the terms of the contract, future business, net profit, or respect for your services. The time you expend, your cash outlay, and your job satisfaction, are typically the units of measure that decide the point at which the rewards become less than the investment.

If you don't get richer and happier from doing something, ask yourself why you're doing the work at all? Perhaps you are acting out of a sense of duty, or feel obliged to return a favor. Only in special cases can there be a justifiable imbalance between reward and output. From time to time we all have to do special favors for our employers and clients, because if we're really honest with ourselves, we ask the same thing of them.

If you are an independent contractor, the meter starts running in the proposal stage of a project. Some clients are indecisive and ask for an inordinate number of ideas for concept; budgets are not firm and require reevaluation and research. This takes time for consultants and, starting with the proposal stage of the project, indicates smaller and smaller net profits. Other clients appear not to understand industry standard pricing. A lack of understanding forces on-going justification for pricing, and diminishes net profits for the consultant. Some clients work in committee, which by nature slows the decision-making process, and can drain a consultant's time and resources before the project even begins.

If you are an employee, your point of diminishing returns can be seen when your employer can't provide a justifiable raise for you; or, can't provide a work environment that allows for growth and creativity. Perhaps your employer is starting to treat you with disrespect.

If a relationship becomes problematic, and requests are unjustifiable, you have to learn to walk away. Here's the formula: if you see that your costs in terms of time, money, and emotion are exceeding your net return in terms of money and satisfaction; if your need for balance and harmony isn't being met; or, if the relationship has negative impact, you have reached your PDR!

You either have to confront your buyer and attempt to make changes, or terminate your participation in the work. That's a very tough decision. But making tough decisions builds character, and character becomes a source of power.

The signals that point towards diminished returns start small and get bigger. Our natural response is to ignore the first few signals. Then there comes a point where you feel mentally exhausted by the time and effort invested (translated into cost) that has made no positive difference in your financial reward or enjoyment. That's the point where a change needs to occur.

Ironically, when you explain to your buyers that the terms of the relationship are becoming problematic for you, and that you need to redefine your participation, your buyer can grow in respect for you. It's hard for a client or an employer to respect a seller who does not value their time or the expense invested in their work. You would think that a buyer would give due consideration to a seller for compromising to meet their needs. But that's not what I've experienced. Human nature seems to react otherwise; many people seem to disrespect 'a giver.'

Buyers respect power. Buyers respect fair and justified parameters, not unlimited access. I'm referring to buyers who are generally fair and respectful people themselves. So I say set your boundaries firmly!

Once you've got the respect of the buyer, the contract written, and the relationship rules obeyed, then throw in something extra at the very end of the deal. A gesture of largesse is appreciated and noted at that time by most buyers, because you're doing it as an act of kindness and appreciation, not as part of the contract. There is a huge difference between doing someone a good turn, and working for less money.

Remember the story "Call the Shots in Your Show" in Ring One? Both the Fat Man and the circus owner experienced diminishing returns. The Fat Man couldn't justify his salary against his health costs. The circus owner couldn't justify charging customers to see a less than humongous fat person. We can learn from the story this lesson: every relationship has a specific set of considerations and parameters that must be met in order for the relationship to be effective. In order to remain in line with those expectations, it is essential to be clear about the goals and needs of the relationship. This means that you'll both be in sync with expectations and with work output. A contract can become a baseline for measuring whether you are fulfilling your obligations, and whether your work is being treated with proper respect.

Getting a grip on diminishing returns will prevent you from getting to a place of no return. It's better to lose a relationship that is imposing than to lose self respect, power, and control.

The Power Myth is Wrong!

The client, the boss, the customer is always right. Power Myth Wrong! If clients were always right, they wouldn't need vendors to counsel them. If employers were always right, they wouldn't need managers to blame things on. Every business owner has heard the mantra that the customer is always right. Sellers (employees, vendor/consultants, retail business owners) live by it and fear it. Yet if sellers live by this creed, sellers will always seed power to buyers (employers, clients, customers) thus creating unequally balanced relationships. Ergo, we have the power myth wrong.

The client needs vendor services in order to realize the client's goals. The same is true of employers and their need for employee services. That's the essence of these relationships. The client/vendor and employer/employee relationships are a fifty/fifty split in need, and a fifty/fifty split in supply. This becomes a fifty/fifty split in power. On the flip side of this equation, sellers want to make money and enjoy the means to a profitable end. Sellers need buyers to reach their financial and career goals, too. Buyers provide income to sellers.

But clients, employers, and retail customers aren't always right in the execution of their decisions and choices. Sometimes, buyers choose unwisely and incorrectly. It is absolutely critical at junctures of disagreement for sellers to clearly understand their role and responsibility in the buyer/seller relationship. Sellers must be educators. Savvy sellers know their product and service better than the buyers. Buyers, whether they cognitively know it or not, rely on the advice and the respectful arguments of sellers to help guide the buyer properly.

An enormous value is placed on the seller who educates without fear. Employees, consultants, and business owners can exercise power and control in their business relationships by fearlessly giving counsel, asking their clients and employers to reconsider their points of view, and by explaining the potentially negative results of a debatable decision. A seller's real value and stock in the buyer/seller relationship is as an educator.

Speak truth to power. Successful employees and vendors who understand the responsibilities of their roles as educators use this concept daily.

Disseminating information that challenges an employer or a client's ideas tests the balance of power in the buyer/seller relationship. When sellers are seen as committed educators, they are drawn closer to the buyer. As buyers seek the counsel of their sellers, buyers have a greater commitment to their sellers. This translates into power and control for the seller, and successful outcomes for the buyers.

Clients and employers need the level of discussion and debate that good employees and vendor/consultants can bring to the relationship. The most powerful people and the most successful people encourage and welcome differing opinions from their staff and team of consultants. Information and logic go a long way with intelligent, open-minded employers and clients. There's a difference between being argumentative and presenting a strong argument.

There's a tricky part to changing this myth. The employer, like the client, does have the last word in decision-making. That's part of their role and responsibility. Employees and vendors can argue a point to a certain extent, but their counsel can only go so far. At some point a final decision must be reached, and that's the buyer's job. This still doesn't mean the buyer is right. And this doesn't put more power on the side of the buyer. This just means that a decision needs to be made. Even a group of two needs a decisive decision-maker. Just think what would have happened if Dave Hoover, the lion trainer, had let the lions and tigers decide when the act was finished. It just wouldn't work.

If you are a consultant or an independent contractor, and your counsel isn't heeded, you have more freedom to decline a project than an employee. You have other clients who will provide a revenue stream if declining a project means that you'll lose the client. If you are a sales representative for a company, your options on declining work vary according to the policies of your company. In any case, you can still offer guidance and you can still play devil's advocate.

Employees are in a more tenuous position than independent contractors. The employee has just one main job to use as a revenue stream and doesn't have a roster of other employers to whom he or she can look for continued revenue enhancement. Even employees have to weigh the options of taking on work that they do not believe is right. Sometimes we have to risk losing our jobs in order to keep our own inner balance of power maintained. We have to do this in a smart way. We cannot put at risk our loved ones who are depending on us financially. We can't neglect paying our bills. But we do have those times when we are challenged to take a stand, make a change, review our own beliefs, and redesign career strategies. Those times generally fall into the category of the big power myth, that someone, not us, is always right. I'd rather restate that phrase this way: the client or employer has the right to be wrong.

Although I was an employee with the circus, I always looked at the circus as my equal partner. I never feared them, and I never worried about disagreeing with them. I bargained hard and would test the boundaries of that relationship at times. As a result, I did not feel powerless in my relationship with the circus. I respected them, and I believe they respected me in return. I'm very grateful for the fact that my employment relationship with the circus had never dissolved because I kept a hard line on my philosophies and positions.

In my post-circus career in the entertainment industry, clients would sometimes ask me to accept unrealistic conditions under which to supply service and product. Without fail each and every time I turned the work down, after good counsel, I never lost the client. But every time I tried to make an unrealistic situation work, I did lose the client.

Promptness & Commitment are the Courtesies of Kings

Promptness and commitment are two ingredients that add up to an enormous amount of respect from employers, clients, and customers. The more respect we get, the more power and control we have in our relationships.

This may sound sophomoric, but a rule of highly successful and respected people is to come to work on time. The easiest way to look like a prima donna: show up late, breezing in a few minutes past the time that everyone is expecting you. Turning up late on a consistent basis is usually perceived by others as a deliberate affront, a negative power move, and is usually highly resented. Prima donnas are the butts of jokes, not the recipients of respect. If your work is excellent, yet you have the habit of consistently showing up late, your work won't be taken as seriously as it should. Just show up on time.

If you are in the habit of consistently arriving a few minutes early, you'll walk on water with your clients and employers. You will be viewed as highly dependable, very respectful of people's time, and you'll be accorded earned power. You'll have power in the bank.

Once at the job on time, stay committed to what you promised you would do. Don't change the work order; don't make substitutions. Do what you contracted to do. There's nothing wrong with doing extra things; that's always appreciated. But don't make preemptive changes to the work that the buyer expects from you.

In the story "Get Creative With Crisis" I would have been screwed if I hadn't arrived on the circus grounds early in Laredo, Texas looking for the hispanic performers for media interviews in Nuevo Laredo, Mexico. Arriving early enabled me to organize a plan B, which was doing the radio interviews myself, masquerading as Spanish-speaking performers. Or, what if I had decided to send someone else in my place to give the performers their instructions, someone who wasn't resourceful and committed to fulfilling the interview obligations—or someone who couldn't speak Spanish? We wouldn't have had the impact across the border with the Spanish-speaking audience, which would have negatively impacted our box office sales.

With the circus, I always kept my standards up for my work. I always arrived early. I had my paperwork organized. I fulfilled the tasks that were required of me. Circus managers could rely on me. Therefore, I constantly kept myself in a strong position of value to the show, so that when I would lobby for a raise, or take a mini-vacation for a late paycheck, I had respect in the bank to use as collateral. I might have been firm in the way that I dealt with the circus at times, but I always delivered a committed work effort.

In the late 80s I moved to Los Angeles and produced music for corporate events as well as for high-end entertainment industry parties, like the Governors Ball post party following the Emmys telecast. The gentleman who hired me to produce my very first Emmy party in 1993 taught me a valuable lesson. Paul Cunliffe, the event organizer, actually changed music producers that year from a vendor who had been involved with that event for many years. As it turned out, our musical presentation was highly successful because the entertainers contracted were top quality. I brought extra staff, arrived early enough to red flag a potential problem, and stuck with the terms of the contract without change. When preparing to leave at the end of the night, Paul came up to me and said that he was extremely pleased with my work because of all the reasons I just mentioned. He said that the formula for success is simple: show up on time and do what you said you were going to do. Promptness and commitment. Ignoring this Performance Tip was the reason why my predecessor lost the business.

Maybe it's easier to remember this lesson through the immortal words of Yogi Bear when giving his philosophy of business manners: " . . . always get to work on time . . . be pleasant to the customers." I try to uphold Yogi's values every day, even though I've returned my Dancing Bear tutu.

The Power Punch

When you want to up your salary, first organize your reasons for a raise, and second ask yourself if these reasons are fair, both to you and the employer. Ask yourself if you have truly earned the right to get more money. Keep in mind that in business, the idea of automatic raises every year is a fairly recent phenomenon, just dating back a few decades. Prior to that time, you only got a raise if you actually justified an increase in salary.

Let's say it's salary review time at your company. You have earned the right to get more money, and you have worked to obtain correct information regarding commensurate salaries at your company and in your industry. Once this is done, don't be afraid to put a value on your services that might be higher than what you're used to earning. Ascertain and position your competitive edge. Frame the talents and skills that you have provided your company over the years; and list other skills you can contribute that would add justification for the raise.

Always position your income request from a point of strength. Know what you're worth to your company; know what you're worth in the industry and marketplace. Understand that you have the freedom to accept or reject the offer. Then go for it. Dig in your heels and negotiate. Nothing can be worse than staying in a job where you feel under compensated and under valued.

Know your point of diminishing returns. Know your exit sign. Be prepared to quit your job if there's no compromise. Money in the bank buys you significant power of decision-making, the freedom to make the best choices, and the power to redirect your career. I cannot stress enough the importance of saving money. When you've got money in the bank, you've got greater freedom to choose.

I once had the experience of negotiating for a post circus job that was a great opportunity for me, and a job that appeared to be a heck of a lot of fun. It was for a public relations position with a teddy bear company. (You can take the girl out of the circus, but you can't take the bear out of the circus girl!) The interview was going great until it came time for salary talk. I came prepared with my salary requirement and support reasons for my price tag.

Before I had a chance to name my price, the interviewer asked me, "How cheap can I get you for?"

Nobody had ever asked me "How cheap can I get you for?" So I was unprepared with a rehearsed response. Because I had already completed many years of turbo negotiating with the circus, forming and shaping the Performance Tools and Performance Tips, I went into immediate Mental Chess and Creative Logic mode and delivered a power punch. The words came tumbling out of my mouth: "Why would you want to get me cheap? The result of me accepting an offer below my justified salary range would hurt both of us in the long run. After the glow of getting hired wears off, I'll start to feel taken advantage of. I'll balk at working more than forty hours a week. You'll expect me to work longer because I am management, and I'll either quit out of a feeling of disrespect, or you'll fire me out of anger. In any case, nobody wins. If you grant me the salary that I've earned through my experience and accomplishments, I'll feel gratified. I'll put in whatever hours are necessary to get the work done, and you'll end up renewing my contract with a raise."

The power punch can effectively be delivered when you understand the buyer/ seller relationship so well that you instantly recognize when an imbalance in the relationship is being presented. You then move in to counter the power blow with logic. Logic is your best weapon against a power blow. It's really hard to beat logic. If the buyer continues to defend an illogical position, head for the door. Call the match. Game over.

The volley paid off. I got the job for the exact salary I requested. I don't know if that company ever again asked a potential employee, "How cheap can I get you for?" I can tell you that they never asked me another question like that for as long as I worked for them.

The Choices We Make Determine Our Fate

Employment at any company is a choice, not a birthright. Employees are not bound forever to their employers. Yet employees stay employed, in fact, go on strike for months to remain employed at companies that either don't want them, or don't value their services commensurately. Many employees are expectant of as many benefits as they can get, like health insurance, vacation time, personal time, and company savings plans in order to join the company. The level of expectation in the employer/employee relationship is out of control.

So why don't people just quit if they don't like their employers, or the nature of the employer/employee relationship? Frankly, it's hard to break away. It's hard to change. It's fearful to leave the comfort zone of a steady paycheck. It can be hard to save enough money to have the financial means to detach from a company and get another job. Intriguingly, those benefits that seemed so attractive when we were hired can become the ball and chain that extend the term of employment beyond what it should be, thus creating dissonance and unhappiness for everyone in the relationship.

If employees looked at themselves as independent contractors, as sellers, they could start positioning their thinking in a different way. Employees/sellers can start to feel more powerful by remembering that they can create options for themselves. Everyone has talents that they can market and sell. No one should feel strapped to a particular job or with a particular client. The longer we stay in a job we don't like, the more unhappiness we create and the more time we waste. Eventually, we're either going to get fired or we're going to quit.

Take charge of change. Be proactive about implementing a change in your career when it's time. Don't fear it; get near it. Change can be fun, exhilarating, and truly productive. Change can be enormously freeing if it gets you to explore other skills and talents that you have. Change in your industry or in your specific job can be the encouragement you need to move forward with a dream you've always wanted to try. Exercising the power of choice will ultimately give you more control over your happiness in your career.

Humility Matters

Be grateful for each piece of business you receive, even when you're tops in your field. Never take anything for granted. Always show up on time for business appointments or activities.

We are at our best, our most pure, our most eager, our most open, and our most likeable when we start a new job, move into a new city, or join a new association. When we have to prove ourselves in a new environment to new people, we typically show humility by being extra nice to people. The problem comes when we become over familiar with an employer, a client, a location, or an association. It has been said that familiarity breeds contempt. I can certainly tell you that familiarity leads to a diminution in humility. Once we start feeling overly familiar with a situation, the all too human condition of ego inflation kicks in. If we remain humble, thankful, and appreciative of what we have built and of what we know, we will constantly express the best aspects of our nature and not the worst.

Humility can be a very powerful tool if harnessed, defined, and measured properly. Humility allows us to keep an open mind with people who have different views than ours. Humility allows us to be appreciative of rewards we receive for the work we do, without being arrogant.

We will be forgiven for mistakes or indiscretions, which we all make, if we maintain humility in our daily posture and stance. In the circus, the Strong Man was a really gentle individual. His sheer size, combined with his soft demeanor, made people warm to him rather than fear him. A perfect example of another such individual is Jesse Ventura, a man who has cultivated a warm and cuddly image, even though he is six feet eight inches tall, and a former pro-wrestler and Navy Seal. He has cultivated an air of approachability, which could be understood as a sense of humility about his great physical gifts. He doesn't take his wrestling persona too seriously, and so everybody likes him, even those who may not agree with his political positions. Jesse Ventura is a hard man to dislike.

Maintaining an attitude of humility allows for our message to get through to our employers and clients. An attitude of humility keeps the channels of communication open instead of creating defensive mental barriers as protective devices. And when we are allowed to voice our thoughts to an audience of accepting ears, we keep our balance of power because we have exercised our voice; we are recognized as a part of the discussion and discourse.

An attitude of pride or a bully's ego cannot sustain healthy, equally balanced relationships. We cannot have balanced relationships if we seek to dominate relationships. Pursuing equally balanced relationships will naturally make you aware of bullying types.

I was a great circus marketing director; so were the other seven. We all successfully promoted shows throughout the United States. Our tent sat 3,500 people; we had two shows a day, three on Saturdays. The marketing directors shouldered a lot of responsibility in regard to generating revenue. My success in such a tough business could have given me a false sense of pride and an inflated ego. But all the marketing directors realized early on that with the best-laid plans and lots of hard work, ticket sales were unpredictable. We all held our breath when it came time for show days. Even with a good advance sale, things could happen that could deter audience attendance. Sometimes it was as simple as a change in the weather.

All the marketing directors were seen as sources of power because our efforts generated revenue. We realized that business could be bad without it being any one person's fault, so we all treated each other less judgmentally than we could have. We all checked our egos at the door, kept an open mind to new ideas, and thanked everyone who helped us. Even on dismal show days with low ticket sales, management and the performers still accorded respect to the marketing team. I swear this is because the marketing directors remained humble in success.

Ironically, humility breeds power.

Ring Three: Performance Tricks

CREATE YOUR CENTER RING ACT

The classified ad in the *Pittsburgh Press* read:

Circus, Circus—See the Country!

> Must have experience in JOURNALISM,
> COMMUNICATIONS, LITERATURE,
> ENTERTAINMENT, BUSINESS MANAGEMENT.
> Must be a self-starter, love to travel,
> ability to work unsupervised.

When I saw this ad in my hometown newspaper, the *Pittsburgh Press*, I immediately knew I was looking at my future—marketing director with a major American traveling circus! Who would have guessed that joining the circus would require the wide range of curriculum choices I made in college. Five years after college graduation, I was rewarded for following my gut instinct, never relinquishing my quest for the perfect job with the perfect lifestyle, which resulted in the greatest career I could imagine.

As can you. The exact job, the specific career path, the series of choices you have to make to get to the work that suits you best is not always evident while in college or immediately following graduation. Life is trial and error, from the courses and majors we choose in college, to the experiments we make with different types of jobs as our careers unfold. You will absolutely know when the right opportunities, with the right supporting lifestyle considerations are presented to you, if you are open to alternative choices, and clear about the aesthetics you want to combine with the skills you want to use.

It's not as though I was a pre-circus major at Duquesne University, my alma mater. In fact, midway through college, like so many students, I found I had to change my major from music to something else, with no concrete idea of the next career choice. I did know that I wanted to live and work in as many places as humanly possible, with as many different cultures of people possible. Surprisingly, the circus seemed to be that strange career choice that utilized the college curriculum I chose—every course of study listed in the classified ad—as well as the lifestyle goals I identified. Later in this chapter, I define the combining of our preferred skills and talents, with work environment preferences, as *workstyle* considerations.

Like many students, I began college with one career goal and finished with an entirely different game plan—or no real game plan at all. Had I not been forced by my father to address my changing career goals and formulate a plan to revise my original career goals, I may have floundered for quite a while longer.

Maybe you had the same conversation with a parent that I did. My father was paying my college tuition, although I was paying for room and board as a resident assistant in my dorm. I was in the second half of my sophomore year of college, and my father sat me down to have The Talk. What were my career goals, he wanted to know.

That was no easy conversation. I had begun college as a music major. I discovered, to my dismay, that I would not be able to compete effectively in the job market in music performance, nor was I interested in the education side of music. I had trained to have some type of career in music since high school. When faced with the reality of what was required to be successful in either music performance or music education, I decided to let go of my dream. I realized it wasn't how I wanted to live my life. My father wanted to know if I had a new career in mind. Frankly, I was wondering the same thing.

I had invested a great deal of time, and my father had invested a great deal of money and time, in that music career, which was over before it began once I hit college. Looking back, I realize it took a high level of self-awareness to acknowledge that although I didn't know the name of the job I wanted, I could tap into the lifestyle and workstyle that I envisioned. Now, training others to develop that high level of self-awareness is an important aspect of my speaking and consulting practice. At that moment, I was just a student who had completed one and a half years of college and had no specific career path in mind. My dad was still waiting for an answer.

I felt unprepared for his question. So I went silent for a few moments, and then I told my father my truth. I didn't know what I would do for work. But I did have a work style path, and I shared that with him: to work with as many different cultures of people possible, and in as many different places in the world as humanly possible. Who knew that would be with the circus?

My father accepted my answer because of his open-mindedness, even though it wasn't what he expected. I was grateful for that.

From the eight years between that conversation with my father and the time I saw that ad in the *Pittsburgh Press*, I got business management experience by running a little nightclub, and by quitting a management training program with a national retailer. Both of these career choices proved incredibly unpopular with my parents, but they should have expected nothing less from a child who quit kindergarten mid-year because it was too boring.

When I saw the circus ad, I suddenly realized that here was my college goal of working with many different cultures of people in many different kinds of places. I immediately applied for that job, and I got it.

What college student would ever think of becoming a marketing director of a major touring circus? The idea certainly had never crossed my mind. As I mentioned earlier, I had never even seen a live circus performance before accepting work for the Clyde Beatty-Cole Bros. Circus. The circus was actually the perfect vehicle for me to achieve the lifestyle choice I had described to my father eight years earlier. I knew how I wanted to live, and that turned out to be much more important than knowing the exact job I would like to do for a living.

I'll never forget my first day of work with the Clyde Beatty-Cole Bros. Circus. It was Niles, Ohio, in June of 1980. As soon as I walked onto the circus grounds, I saw a group of little costumed chimpanzees holding hands, walking single file into the Big Top, led by their trainer. They were so cute and sweet that I did what anybody would do in that situation.

I smiled.

Wrong thing to do.

Instantly, those sweet, cute, chimpanzees were enraged. They broke rank and started running toward me, to attack me! I had only been with the circus for a matter of minutes, and now I was about to be devoured by baby chimpanzees? What was happening? Why did these little furry creatures, dressed in sailor suits and hats, hate me? It made no sense. Later, with order restored and a little damage done to my vanity, the trainer explained to me that my smile had been the cause of the problem. For a chimpanzee, a smile is an act of declared war. When they bare their teeth, they are giving their battle cry. Who knew I had set off a signal to fight? Certainly not I.

I learned my first lesson in working with other cultures; cultural diversity being one of two workstyle goals I set for myself in college. And, yes, chimpanzees constitute a culture all their own. They were so adorable in their outfits, off to work, holding hands, looking precious. Except that looks are deceiving. Every culture has its own language. Body movements and facial expressions have different meanings specific to cultures and species. I had to learn the chimpanzees' language. They weren't going to learn mine. I also had to learn their trainer's language, which was French. And that was a lot tougher than learning to speak chimpanzee.

You'd think my senses would have been on the alert in regard to cultures and signals when the next animal act took the stage. It was the circus bear troupe. Alas, I had not. Imagine my delight. It's day one of my circus career and I've just survived an onslaught of angry chimpanzees, when all of a sudden, an enormous grizzly bear (or some kind of really big bear) comes charging in my direction. So what do I do this time?

You guessed it. I smiled. Then I froze.

More specifically, I screamed and froze, thinking the bear knew I was a First of May (a circus term for a brand new convert to circus life) and decided to attack me as a new snack! Make no mistake about circus animals. They may look docile at times, but they're certainly not tame. These are wild animals with enough training to pose more than a minimal threat to their trainers and to the audience. Circus animals are wild and dangerous beasts. I was about to learn another lesson in communication, but this time the joke was *really* on me!

If you speak Spanish, you can make yourself understood in Italian, because the languages have a number of words and phrases in common. The same, I discovered, can be said of the languages of bears and chimpanzees. While sometimes these animals may need translators in order to make themselves fully understood, it turns out that a smile means about the same thing to a bear that it does to a chimpanzee. It means that you are showing your resolve to fight, and that you are threatening an attack.

The bear situation was a little different. The chimpanzees misunderstood me, but *I* misunderstood the bear. My close encounter of the furred kind (sorry, couldn't resist!) took place during a live performance, with about 3,500 people looking on.

What happened was, I was standing between center ring, where the bear act was taking place, and the elevated stage where the band played. I didn't see the empty cage positioned in center ring, near where I stood, strategically placed for the bear to lumber over, open it, get in, all as part of the act. This was designed to scare people, because the bear appeared to be "on the loose." I had never seen the act before; I had just experienced my run-in with the chimpanzees. I thought the bear was coming over to attack me!

I screamed and backed up into the bandstand, purse and training manual flying out of my grasp, while the band showed me *their* teeth. They were laughing their heads off. I could have suffered a concussion. I definitely suffered an ego blow. Now the bear *could* have killed me if I had met him on the street and smiled at him, but just not right then. Between the bear act and the chimp trainer, my first day at the circus could have been my last day on earth.

I think I endeared myself to the circus staff through my calamities, although I later learned that this sort of thing is typical, at least with the chimps. Almost everybody has to learn the hard way not to smile at the chimps, no matter how cute they may be; and not to run screaming from the bear act. Later on, whenever I used the bear act to pose for interviews with media and contest winners, I always kept my distance. And I never smiled. It was hard to make people understand that these were still wild animals. I guess people thought that circus animals had been trained to be a hundred percent docile all the time. They aren't. Just ask Siegfried & Roy. Call me a sissy if you will, but my job was to get the circus into the newspaper, not myself into the obituaries. So I always kept my distance from wild circus animals, big and small.

My third memory of day one of my circus career resulted in a much happier outcome. It, too, began with a smile. This time, I was smiling not at a wild animal but at a circus band member, Clarke Weigle, my future short-term husband. Clarke was part of an eight-piece brass band that traveled with the circus. He played the euphonium, the musical instrument resembling a baby tuba. We met in front of the hot dog concession truck on the Midway. He was standing in his tuxedo, watching Jim the Sideshow Barker pitching the audience, while waiting for the evening performance to begin. I introduced myself and told him I thought I knew him from somewhere. We played mental geography and thought of all the people, dates, and places we might possibly have in common. It turns out that we couldn't connect through any prior event we could think of. Still, I had this incredible sense that I knew him. And as Jane Austen wrote, I (eventually) married him.

All of these stories are important because I felt completely at home with the circus, in lieu of near fatal animal tragedies. Yes, I ran into serious, possibly life threatening situations, first with the chimpanzees and then with the bear. But I survived those moments, rolled with the punches, and eventually became friends with the very same animal trainers who scoffed at me on my first day of work. I connected with the job—marketing director with a major American traveling circus—that embodied my primary workstyle goals. Five years after college graduation and several jobs later, I felt I was where I needed to be.

The opportunity to be at one with your work, to experience the joy and fulfillment of a job or a business that is an extension of your natural instincts, talents, and lifestyle goals, is available to everyone. You must first of all understand that you're going to make choices for earning income through your choice of work anyway; your choices can either be a compromise to a perfect lifestyle, or a perfect fit. Let's see how to do this.

Workstyle Your Goals

Who says your job has to be cookie-cutter?

Or that you have to make normal career choices? Who says you can't create a brand new job category in your target industry? Any reason why you can't choose a career that is an extension of your ideal lifestyle, rather than have your job dictate your lifestyle? The first rule of creating your center ring act is to make your own rules. The key here is: *define how you want to live; envision the types of people with whom you want to associate; and, use your favorite skills and talents.*

This isn't a completely new concept. Society's artists—actors, painters, and musicians—have lived like this since the dawn of time. Their lifestyle is integral to their career. They live a *workstyle* that is balanced between the way they like to work and the actual work itself. But now it's time for the rest of us—employees, business owners, and consultants—to unshackle ourselves from outdated notions and limitations when choosing career paths.

You and I face the same issues on our paths to finding fulfilling work and building a fulfilling life. We want a job that we love doing, one that creates a lifestyle we love living. The blending of work and lifestyle is our *workstyle*. Many people, while in college and even after graduation, still aren't sure of exactly what job they want. They can end up choosing jobs based on parental expectations, college career counselors' guidance, current listings of preferred jobs, or, by falling into something their friends are doing. Few people can really know what job they will love doing until they do it. Workstyle goals will help to focus and guide you towards selecting the job that fits your lifestyle.

On the other hand, I think most people of any age have a better understanding about how they want to live their lives than the specific job they want. If just asked. Work notwithstanding. We know intrinsically how we would like to live, the kinds of hobbies or avocations we would like to pursue, the kinds of people we want to be with, the importance of travel in our lives, and so on. In other words, people are much more certain of the kind of lifestyle they wish to lead rather than the kind of career they think they ought to follow. But people aren't counseled to choose lifestyle first. Therefore, most people aren't geared towards workstyle choices.

People just aren't taught or encouraged to think lifestyle over work. It seems to be emblematic of American work philosophy that lifestyle should be sacrificed in our career choices. I think there should be more time and counseling given to workstyle before job consideration. Or, we end up having a life that isn't as fulfilling as it could be.

Colleges will bring in career counselors to help students evaluate job selection, but when was the last time that a lifestyle counselor was brought in to work with students? Let's change the rules of how people choose their work paths by dealing with lifestyle considerations to support workstyle goals.

Corporations will hire outplacement services to help recycle workers who are being laid off if the company is downsizing or restructuring. These outplacement firms are geared towards redistributing workers into similar jobs in similar industries. As tough as the transition period is for the soon-to-be-laid-off employee, it's also the best time to revise the standard and typical way of formulating a continuing career path. No matter the age, it's never too late to establish a work opportunity using the workstyle approach towards career building.

I didn't consciously push my career in the direction of circus work. Instead, I made decisions about the kind of workstyle I wanted instead of the actual job I wanted. After eliminating music as a career option in college, I had no idea what to do. I was unprepared to define a new career path through a job category.

My first meaningful career choice, marketing director for the Clyde Beatty—Cole Bros. Circus, didn't occur until five years after graduation. I didn't choose that job out of a childhood fantasy to join the circus. I recognized, while reading the classified ad in the *Pittsburgh Press*, that working for a traveling circus would be the fulfillment of the workstyle goals I had made in college. The job found me. It turned out that working for the circus also used all of the skills and talents that I had explored and enhanced while in college. It became the fulfillment of my ideal workstyle vision.

So the question now becomes this: How can you make a workstyle choice that will give you joy and excitement, and establish a true connection between your lifestyle needs and your favored talents? We go back to the key and break it down: *define how you want to live; envision the types of people with whom you want to associate; and, use your favorite skills and talents.* First, define how you want to live. Don't make this too complicated. What is your first reaction when this question is posed: How do I want to live? Aspects of that decision can include the amount of adventure you need in your life;

the amount of change you prefer; the place that money holds in relation to adventure; and the comfort of familiarity. But the point is that the decision needs to be instantaneous. In *Blink* by Malcolm Gladwell the author discusses the importance of intuitive decision-making. Gladwell supports the position that people intuitively know how to get to the best answers to questions they face without a lot of information cluttering the decision process. When asked how you want to live, what's the first thing that comes to mind? Whatever that answer is, is the answer to consider. It doesn't matter if the answer is as simple as lots of interaction with people versus very little human contact. The relevant issue is that it's your answer. And your gut response is the truth by which you should live.

Second, envision the types of people with whom you want to associate. The types of people you put in your life through your work will define and enrich your life in a specific way. The essence of our enjoyment in life is the way in which we interact with the people. We are defined by our choices in life, and the people we choose to have around us define who we are. These people will bring experiences and joy to your life equal to their outlook on life. Your life will be shaped and influenced by the people surrounding you.

Third, choose and use your favorite skills and talents. Skills and talents can either be aesthetic or functional. We are either people committed to service; or we're people committed to organization and development. Sometimes, you just have to continue to explore and use talents and skills without a clear direction. The first two parts of the workstyle hunt are the most important to define. This third part should be an on-going exploration of things that we find fascinating, and things that are natural behavior patterns that we exhibit each day.

If you continue to investigate subjects of interest and of aptitude to you, and trust your gut responses in terms of naming the manner in which you want to live your day and the people with whom you want to fill your day, you will reach your perfect workstyle.

Workstyle is the foundation for harmony and balance in your professional life. Statistics show that most people do not have financial reward as the top incentive for choosing their careers or their jobs. Compensation is important, but enjoyment at work holds a greater priority. Most people want their employers to let them blend work with family life.

My run-ins with the chimps, the bear, and Clarke Weigle, my future shortterm husband, all on that first day on the job, gave me an exhilarating sense that I was in exactly the right place at exactly the right time. I knew that

I didn't want to be anywhere else than where I was right then, in Niles, OH as marketing director with the Clyde Beatty-Cole Bros. Circus. How many of us can say as much about our jobs or career choices? Working with a company, or having a business that is in sync with your aesthetic goals and needs is magnificent. It's energizing; it's freeing; and it's so much fun.

Idea Energy helps us to choose a career that is enjoyable, rewarding, and somehow educational. It begs us to ask the fundamental questions: How do I want to live? Who do I want to be? What sort of life do I want to lead? Or, how do I turn this clown car called my career around?

It turned out that all the talents and skills that I had explored and studied in college, through a series of six declared majors (my parents deserve awards for patience and understanding), paid off handsomely, five years after graduation. With the circus job I used my communications courses by working with the media and participating in interviews. My communication skills helped me to eventually learn to speak enough chimpanzee and bear to get through the day without the risk of being mauled! My Spanish language training became helpful with the hispanic population on the circus, and when we were marketing to Hispanic audiences. I used my journalism courses by writing press releases for the circus. I used my English literature studies to find and express deeper meanings in my public relations stories. My background as a musician factored into forming great relationships with the circus band; I was invited to play piccolo on a recording of the Clyde Beatty-Cole Bros. Circus band, under the direction of maestro Merle Evans from The Ringling Bros. Barnum & Bailey Circus, the greatest circus bandleader in the world. And I used my philosophy studies to develop sales and marketing strategies. Most people think that philosophy has no actual relationship to the real world. By studying philosophy, I learned how to think through conflicts with employers, clients, and employees so as to resolve them with fair and well-balanced results.

In our society, we tend to put things backwards. First we figure out what we want to do, and only eventually, if ever, do we get around to the questions of who we want to be, and how we would actually like to live our lives. Too often, we look at jobs or careers in narrow terms: the salary, the benefits, vacation time, but we don't focus on what it would mean to live a life dedicated to that sort of endeavor. Millions of people go to law school without ever having the slightest idea of what it is that lawyers do. It's no wonder there are so many unhappy lawyers! Countless people go to work for corporations, attracted by the perks and the promised prestige. But do they have any concept of what corporate life is like? Are they aware of the competitiveness and gamesmanship that such jobs can entail? Doubtful. And that's why there are so many round pegs in square holes.

We have to understand our lifestyle needs before we can know the work to choose. I want to suggest that instead of focusing first on the kind of job you're after, we should focus on the kind of life that we want to lead. If I hadn't worked out in my mind the aesthetics of how I wanted to live my work life while still in college, my eye would never have been attracted to the circus want ad for marketing director in the classified section of the *Pittsburgh Press*, my hometown newspaper. After all, I wasn't one of those people who fell in love with the circus at age six and knew that I always wanted to run off and join one. I had never been to a circus before that day when I annoyed the chimpanzees, freaked at the bear, and met my temporary future husband. Instead, I knew how I wanted to live, and when the time was right, I discovered what I could do in order to make that desired lifestyle possible.

In other words, I'm one of the few people who have been equally influenced by the philosophies of Plato, Schopenhauer, and Bubbles the Clown! I am here to share that expertise with you.

Follow Your Heart

The next step towards designing your unique workstyle, is to fearlessly follow your heart. We have many talents, skills, and areas of interest that we can use in our careers. Think about how you played as a child. Think about the way you related to your friends while growing up. Try to recall how you interacted with adults in your youth. Are there things that you did while you were playing that could be converted into a job or business? Are there behavior patterns you can look back upon that can be converted into work?

I know of an individual, Dan Duquette, who did a series of exercises during his senior year of college that asked essentially these same questions. What did he like to do in his playtime? Play baseball. What did he do in the summers? Play baseball. What did he like to read about when he wasn't doing schoolwork? You guessed it, baseball.

While all his college classmates were applying to law and business schools for continuing education, Dan Duquette sent out resumes to all of the professional major league baseball teams. All but one rejected him, but life is not about your batting average, even if you want to work in baseball! He got a job as an assistant scout for one team. Three years later, he was promoted to full time scout, and two years later, to assistant general manager of a different team. Within eight years of graduation from college, this same individual was one of the youngest general managers in the major leagues, commanding a salary of three-quarters of a million dollars a year.

All because he loved baseball, and all because it never seriously crossed his mind that making a living involved surrendering all of his childhood dreams and pleasures. The main thing is to base your career plans on the things that gave you the most pleasure as a child, while you were growing up. Those are most likely to be the same things that give you pleasure as an adult.

If you've done a one eighty from your childhood and surrendered all the things that gave you joy and pleasure as a child; if you're not happy with the work you're doing now, try taking a trip down memory lane. Better yet, ask your siblings and your childhood friends how they remember you as a kid. It can be enlightening and surprising to hear your life told back to you by the people who grew up with you. Take the childhood photo albums out to help jog your memories. This can be one of the best voyages you can take to refocus on your future. (If you hate your childhood pictures, just stick to querying your friends and family.)

In my case, one of the things I loved was to put on shows in our garage when I was eight years old. I took the neighborhood kids and organized them into a little theatre group. I produced music variety shows featuring my friends as the performers. We would lip-synch to the songs played on my phonograph. (If you're under thirty, a phonograph is . . . well, never mind!)

I would then promote the shows with fliers that were distributed to the neighbors. I charged admission to the shows. I even asked the kids' mothers to bake cookies for us so that we could sell them as concession items at the show in order to generate additional revenue to continue to produce more shows.

It's probably not a coincidence that I ended up in show promotion with the circus. After marrying the circus bandleader and establishing residency within the circus community, I repeated my biggest childhood activity—I created the Children's Theatre Company. I needed a personal identity for myself, so I did it by what came naturally to me as a kid—organizing people and making theater. If we allow ourselves to follow our hearts, our instincts, and our loves, we would create a workstyle that provides perfect harmony for our happiness.

I was really surprised to hear my sister, Jeri, and my oldest friend, Lisa Cooper Jensen tell me what I was like when I was young. Lisa remembers the concept of logic being integral to my ability to accept life situations. She told me about conversations we had while waiting for the school bus in the morning, as far back as elementary school, discussing the logic of news stories, religious teachings, and parental disciplinary actions. She even reminisced about kindergarten, recalling the logic I used with my parents, that my time could be better spent on my own, making crafts and creating organized activities with my neighborhood friends than participating in imposed school activities like nap time.

My sister Jeri remembers the actual pitch I made to my parents about dropping out of kindergarten, and detailing the type of group activities and schedule of events I had planned if able to change my daily routine to one that was more entrepreneurial—for a five year old. She also remembers the incredulous look on my parents' faces when I was presenting the plan. This recollection was important because it showed a natural proclivity toward self-expression, debate, salesmanship, and entrepreneurship. When I joined the circus I always said that the job I had, marketing a series of individual towns, and being responsible for generating revenue in those towns, was like having my own business. The experience was a recreation of my childhood activities, like my neighborhood garage shows.

So too, when I conduct workshops and seminars now, it's done as a show, with musical accompaniment and audience interaction. I used all of my natural instincts and work experiences to form the current era of my career.

Self-evaluation of your childhood, along with an evaluation of the things that turn you on and the things you naturally do repetitively, will help you know your heart and choose work that is an outlet for your personality.

RE/INVENTION TECHNIQUES

Create a Career Adventure

Whether choosing a career for the first time, reinventing a career in progress, or reentering the job market after raising children, the approach is the same. The *first* step is to define the aesthetics of your workstyle: define the level of adventure you want, the environment that intrigues you, and the type of people with whom you want to interact. Do you want to travel? Do you want a lot of change in your life? In general, decide how you would like to live your day through your work. You can't have the perfect job if you don't have your aesthetic goals in order and defined.

The *second* step is to evaluate your goals: decide if you want to leave a mark on society. What would you like to contribute to your chosen industry, to your community, and to the world? Ask yourself where your personal goals fit with your career goals: Do you want to marry and have a family, or spend more time on your career? Your career is a movement through time that pays you money for effort invested in someone's goals. But how much of that invested time, thought, and energy underscore your goals? Beyond being good at what you've chosen to do for work, and negotiating a salary that is acceptable to you, do you have a purpose and a reason for the work you're doing?

The *third* step is to understand your identity: How best to express yourself through the work you choose? There are dreams inside of all of us that consistently come to the surface. These dreams are our identities. So often, though, we dismiss our dreams as non-realities. Or, we identify ourselves through someone else's eyes, while using someone else's perceptions of who we are and what we could/should be doing. The people familiar with us since childhood can help us remember the way we behaved in the developing stages of our lives, and to recall the activities in which we excelled in our youths.

Contrary to what you may read in other books on career guidance, do not write this down! Do not make a list! Just think and say who you want to be and what you want to do, even if just aesthetically. Lists can be confusing and can take you outside of yourself. Lists can be confining if an unusual job is the thing that suits you best. You may not be able to put yourself in a category yet. The exact job may not be obvious, but the types of things you find yourself naturally doing will be obvious. We all have natural tendencies that surface in our daily lives. Those things can be the foundation for your career. So just think; just be silent. Let your feelings come to the surface. Then say how you want to live, and say how you want to work. This is soul-searching versus job searching. And if, like Dan Duquette, you have a passion that just won't quit, that passion may be your ticket to your most fulfilling career.

Then you can evaluate elements around you to create a career adventure. If you're in college, look at the types of electives you've been taking. What do you find yourself drawn to? Perhaps your career can be found in your electives rather than your major. If you've declared a major, are you excited about the work and can you see yourself wanting to do that work every day? If you are currently working and need to make a change, extract those elements from your job that you like, that are relevant, and see if they can be redirected in another way within your industry. More than likely there is a need in your industry that no one else is addressing. Conceivably you are disenchanted with your work, and can use your disenchantment as the basis for a new job or a new business. Maybe you never thought seriously about going into business for yourself, but perhaps this is a logical next step for you.

If you are reentering the workforce as a mother who has raised children and now has fewer demands on personal time, I bet you don't realize the skills you've amassed in your role as a mom that you can position, frame, market, and turn into a career. Catching up with technology, probably the biggest on-going change in the business world, isn't as hard as you might think, and that's the biggest obstacle you'll face. The world is still the same—people dealing with and needing people. As a mother, you become a diplomat of people in order to survive and raise your family.

The *fourth* and last aspect of developing a career adventure is waiting. Defining your workstyle, developing your identity, and choosing skills and talents that lay a foundation for a career, all need time to gel and materialize. You have to experiment with jobs, poke around the job market and see what's out there, launch a small business, and do whatever you have to do to get started. Time will be your unit of measure that will bring your thoughts and your efforts together. Remain committed to your dreams and you will be able to create the career adventures that will always fulfill you.

Frame and Position Your
Skills and Talents

Your skills and talents are a part of you forever. Throughout your life you can apply them differently and with different goals. Your choices are endless. And you always have the option to make as many new choices with your skills and talents as you want.

Ask yourself this question: If I had to choose just one skill or talent upon which to build my career, what would it be? Then consider how to apply that talent, either in the industry in which you are currently working, or in an industry that you find more appealing. After a fulfilling career with the circus, and in pursuit of the next big career adventure, my answer to that question was "talking." The one skill and talent I wanted to use was talking—on the phone, in groups, on the radio, on television, and in CD format. That's why I decided to become an author and a speaker, because I absolutely love talking.

In order to make one choice, with one skill that would make you the happiest, and provide for you a great income, you are actually putting yourself in a perfect position to find the center of your happiness. This exercise forces you to strip your life down to the very essence of what makes you come alive, and what really turns you on. What would it be that you would love to do all day?

After determining the skill you are going to market and sell, the next step is to position and frame the skill. Sometimes, we aren't even aware of the skills and talents we possess that are marketable, unique, and in demand. I include in this category even those social skills or domestic skills that we typically would not think could be used in order to earn a living. For example, women who are in charge of the family's finances can use this skill to work as a bookkeeper in a business. Debbie Fields, a stay-at-home mom who wanted to start her own business, started Mrs. Field's Cookies. She used her skill of baking and started a nationwide business. You might be surprised at the skills and talents you have that can be converted into assets in your work life!

Even if you kiddingly said "read fashion magazines" as your one talent to choose for a career, that would indicate a desire for the fashion industry, and possibly a job in the administrative or writing staff of a fashion periodical. Perhaps you have a special area of interest within the fashion industry that can be used for a career, like photography, accessorizing, fashion styling, or personal shopping. You could bring objectivity and innovation to the fashion industry that an insider may be missing. Positioning and framing the thing you like to do the most can result in a wonderful career path.

The trick is to identify the things you do well, then frame and position those things within the needs of the business world. Since the needs of business change with technology, and with economic growth, it's important to feel comfortable with non-traditional approaches toward career choice and toward marketing yourself. Positioning and framing can help you take a hobby, or something you simply find you enjoy on a personal level, and turn it into a lucrative and highly enjoyable career. Talk about feeling a sense of power and control over your lives, this is it!

Work Through Fear of Change

Who doesn't fear change? Career change puts you into an arena of unknown factors. What are the obstacles you'll be facing in your new career endeavor? How do you know you'll be successful? What if nobody wants you or recognizes your value? What if people laugh at you because you're bad at this new thing? And worst of all, what if you can't make money and become homeless? (My single greatest fear is homelessness.)

In "Innovation Rattles Cages" I described how I hid in the bushes for three days before I mustered the courage to get on the elephant and try to be part of the elephant act? Well, you'll probably never be asked to mount the back of an elephant as part of a job interview, which is one of the things I had to do when I was reinventing my life as a performer on the circus. I came out of the bushes, faced my fear of physical agility, and got on the elephant. Even though I didn't end up riding the elephant for more than five minutes, the experience of facing my fear certainly increased my sense of strength and power. I felt better about myself, because I demonstrated that I had the courage to do a very scary thing.

Just think of it this way: experiencing fear (the new "F" word) is the first step towards success if you confront your fear and work through it. The process is simple: go ahead and be fearful. Go ahead and hide a bit from the fear. Then go back and study the specific thing that makes you fearful. Look at your worst-case scenario if failure is imminent. Make a plan B to thwart that worst-case scenario if it actually happens. Then just agree to fear, so that you can face your fear, eliminate it, and move forward with your new career adventure.

If you're looking for a career adventure that has absolutely no fear involved, look no further . . . it doesn't exist. Anything worth undertaking is worth fearing. Even if you instinctively know that your new career/job choice is right, fear can still creep into your behavior and stall your progress. Just know that part of the price successful people pay for their accomplishments is the effort involved in overcoming fear.

I referred to the barons of change a little earlier in Ring One: "Performance Tools" when talking about the excitement you can feel when your work has to change. The barons of change are some of the richest people in the world. They mastermind change. They change society because they love change. This is probably their big skill and talent manifested in the industry they have chosen as a vehicle for creating change. So the barons of change are the catalysts for some degree of your fear.

You can use change to think ahead and develop a change of your own in any industry. You can be a baron of change. You can capitalize on change. You can either respond to, or invent change that results in a lot of enjoyment, and by the way, mucho dinero.

The scariest thing is letting fear rule your choices.

MARKETING YOURSELF

Network to Build Business

The easiest and fastest way to market yourself is by joining associations within all related industries to your work. There's an association for everything. Most importantly, identify your buyers and join networking associations that specifically exist for the education of your buyers. Join every association where you are a vendor to the core group of the association, the buyers. The reason you want to be a vendor to the core group is to make your membership and your time convert into dollars. Your goal is to hobnob with buyers and clients, people who can spend money on your product or services. If you join associations where you represent the core group, the association becomes an educational vehicle; you'll be mixing with your competitors and not with your potential buyers. There's nothing wrong with this, but networking with other competitors just won't convert into dollars as fast.

Here is the key to using associations successfully: *carve an identity for yourself in the group by volunteering for projects or for a role that is the hardest to fill.* Volunteering in associations accomplishes several goals: it endears you to people because you're participating in the success of the organization; and it gives you an added identity beyond what you do for a living. Volunteering for projects also gives you a reason to talk to people at the monthly mixers instead of just making sales pitches for your company. People then get to know you as a multi-faceted person. This is a form of "soft-selling," and can be a most valuable tool if used properly. You're selling yourself as a person first, which will eventually entice people to want to talk with you about your work.

As if volunteering for tough assignments isn't enough, I advise that you try to get on the board of directors. A board position will give you the appearance of power and allow you to network with other powerful people within your related industry. When people see you as powerful, they really want to do business with you.

In Los Angeles, several years after leaving the circus, I started producing bands and orchestras for private parties such as weddings, fundraisers, and conventions for my brother's company, West Coast Music Services. A core base of buyers for our product line, live entertainment, were catering and sales executives with hotels, and corporate event and meeting planners who would be asked by their clients to design large events, including the entertainment components. I called professionals in these above-mentioned categories and asked about the associations to which they belonged. I then joined every one of them. After joining, I asked the board of directors of each association if there were areas of need that I could fill as a volunteer, like writing for the association newsletter, or working as a greeter at the monthly meetings. My plan was to volunteer for the jobs that were the hardest to fill and increase my value to the organization even more. I was looking for anything that would put me in the spotlight in front of the membership, and give me an identity separate and apart from my role as a live music producer.

Within a year of joining every association, I was asked to run for positions on the boards of directors. The increase in my sales for West Coast Music Services was parallel to the awareness I developed for myself as a representative of the company.

Be Buyer Knowledgeable

Learning everything about *your* industry is something I expect you're going to do. I certainly hope you will, because knowledge provides power. I suggest you take the power of knowledge and learn everything you can about your *buyers'* industries. Knowing your buyers' desires, concerns, and limitations will allow you to talk with them as one of their peers. When you approach them with solutions to upcoming problems, you start writing your own ticket for success, because people *love* people with ideas and solutions—especially if it keeps their costs down and profits up. If you use change, and it's cousin, Idea Energy as catalysts for growth, you will definitely gain the respect of your employers and clients. With their respect comes their business; and that's what it's all about!

There was a 1988 movie called *Working Girl* that starred Melanie Griffith, Sigourney Weaver, and Harrison Ford. Melanie Griffith was cast as Tess McGill, a young, smart, enterprising secretary to Sigourney Weaver, a ruthless, upwardly mobile corporate executive who allowed her ego to set her up for careless behavior. Weaver's undoing was her outdated buyer knowledge, and Melanie's aggressive pursuit of current buyer knowledge, for their company's biggest client. Weaver's character let her edge slip, while Griffith's character eventually received Weaver's position at the company because she stayed on top of the growing needs of that client, and presented a solution to a pending problem that nobody else saw. Tess McGill had superior buyer knowledge and used it to promote herself.

Once I became a part of the circus industry, I read everything I could about the American circus, circuses internationally, and the history of the combined Clyde Beatty and Cole Bros. circuses, so that I would be better able to do my job. Gathering historical information about the circus industry, as well as individual acts, allowed me to write more creative press releases, which led to more and better media interviews, which generated bigger box office grosses. I wanted to be an expert in the field of circus business because I wanted my employer to respect me. I anticipated that this would raise my monetary value to them, and that it did.

When I was the Dancing Bear, I studied the movements of the bears on our show so that I could move convincingly in the ring. I went to the point of studying Yogi Bear cartoons, too, so that I could gain insight into this famous fictional bear's behavior and comically reference what the general public typically knew of bears. I could make a "smarter than the average bear" joke here, but I will respect your intelligence and refrain!

Showing my circus employer that I learned and understood the circus industry allowed me to engage in tough salary negotiations, lobby for the Halloween Show continuance, break gender tradition to work with the roustabouts, retain my job when I let Bubbles the Clown go to jail, and all because I came from a position of knowledge, of hard work, and of results and success. Knowledge of your buyers' industries leads to a strong and balanced relationship with them; and gives you the ability to help grow in your business and career with firmer control.

Truly understand what your buyer is looking for, and what your buyer wants to avoid. Giving buyers both what they want, and what they don't think they need, is intrinsic to the long-term success of the employer/ employee and the client/ vendor relationships. Employers and clients need people who think alongside them, for them, and bring to the table a level of thinking that at the very least challenges them. It shows them that you have common goals and that you care about the success of the company, the success of your relationship with them, and your personal success, too. If you are participatory in targeting areas for change and growth, as a result of your buyer awareness, you will make yourself invaluable to them.

Practice Personal Public Relations

Successful people promote themselves. They make themselves visible and vocal wherever they go. You have to be your own ringmaster if you want to be a player in your industry. You have to promote yourself as an individual. It's hard for many people to promote themselves personally, to be that casually confident, in control person at a networking meeting. But it can be easier than you think. You can call attention to your center ring acts without offending people's sensibilities. You don't have to turn into the obnoxious self-promoters we run screaming from, people who can't even hold the attention of a cocktail crowd hungry for witty witticisms.

Beyond the traditional methods of business marketing—advertising, promotion, and publicity—you can promote yourself in six easy ways. *First* is by volunteering to help with fundraising organizations. By lending your professional knowledge and expertise to a nonprofit group, you are helping a worthy cause and soft-selling your services, too. Business opportunities can easily come from working on a fundraiser. While preparing and organizing for an event, you get to know about the personal and professional sides of your co-volunteers. People like doing business with people they get to know in an environment that's tangential to their core businesses.

Second is through networking meetings where you can casually reference situations and experiences that you had to handle in your work. Just be understated about it and make sure there's a learning lesson attached to the story. People love information and learning lessons that they can use for themselves; they'll listen to a brief self-promotion story if the payoff is about furthering their causes and enlightening their lives.

Third self-promotion technique is to engage buyers in conversations and debates about issues affecting their industries. You would be serving as a catalyst for conversation—a much-needed role even in purely social groups. A catalyst is normally accorded leader status, if you're not obnoxious about it. People look up to leaders; buyers are always looking for unique ideas and forward-thinking people. This is a great way to get recognition in conversation circles.

Fourth, when attending a professional seminar, put your hand up and introduce yourself and your business; ask questions and make comments. In a gathering like a seminar, you have an available audience. Take advantage of that by sharing your ideas with the group through the questions you ask, and the comments you make. Give a bit of your philosophy on the subject at hand, while you're at it. It shows depth of thinking and a pioneer attitude.

Fifth is a seldom-used personal public relations habit I learned from Deane Allen, a former employer who was Director of the Sarasota Opera Association. She taught me to write short notes of congratulations to people who are featured in the news. Only the most successful people think of doing this, especially to someone they may not know. Successful people want to interact with other successful people, and take steps towards approaching them. This habit of note writing, without asking for anything but a general desire to meet that person someday, shrouds you in an air of confidence. It's not hard to find addresses for people who have profile pieces written about them because their companies are generally listed. Oh, and Diane Sawyer, if the legend is correct, writes her notes in longhand. That puts an extra special touch to the personal public relations gesture.

Sixth is the toughest of all personal public relations skills because it requires time—return all phone calls from people who want to be vendors to you. I learned this from Mo Austin, former Director of Artists & Repertoire with Warner Bros. Records. I read a beautiful article on Mr. Austin in the *Los Angeles Times* many years ago that detailed his habits of success. One of the most important things was Mo's commitment to returning all his artists' (vendors to a record company) phone calls. His legend was that he showed that he valued everybody by returning their calls. Plus, I expect, that Mo knew that in order to stay competitive in your industry, you always have to be open to new information. It's one thing to establish on-going relationships with vendors you like and with whom you feel a strong level of comfort; it's another thing to rule out new information from people who are trying to tell you about themselves through the introductory phone call. You've lost your competitive edge when you put up a wall of silence with new vendor calls. The people you're ignoring today could be the people who rise to the top of their industries tomorrow, and give you the silent treatment back when you try to approach them.

You always have daily opportunities to call attention to your work, your ideas, and to you as a person. The circus could've put anybody in the bear suit that I eventually came to wear. Since it was my bear suit, I tried to make myself the best and most valuable bear I could be. (A bear with a college degree is still pretty unusual to me!) I sent word around the circus for performers to come into the tent and check out new tricks I developed for the bear character. Pretty soon, the bear became an icon of amusement, and the animated animal act, of which I proudly became a part, got a lot of respect from the real performers. It was an unbearably good time in my life. (Couldn't resist!)

Change Your Game

Your relevance in the business world changes as a result of new technology, an upheaval in the economy, and, whether we like to admit it or not, our own age! Change is ever present. So beat change to the punch. Work ahead of the trends. Evaluate your skills and your interests with an eye for new applications for your products or services. An essential key to success in a changing business world is to create increasing and new demands for your talents, your products, or your services.

Let's look at the steps you can take to reinvent your role within your current industry. *First,* as you see changes that threaten your job and your income, get ready to reposition and reframe your work to address those changes. *Second,* evaluate the reason for the change. *Third,* consider the aspects of your job that are still vital to your industry and enjoyable for you. *Fourth,* look at new demands created by this industry change and retool to meet those changes. If you can identify the change, and create a solution, you have dealt with change in a profitable way.

Changing your game plan is important. It's the difference between being irrelevant in your industry and career, and being a visionary. The good news about change is that it forces you to be resilient, and to offer the business world more and more of your abilities. Understand that you always have skills and talents that aren't being tapped. Activating these untapped talents will always help you breathe life into your career.

Don't wait until your department is given its pink slip. You can be the innovator, the prophet of reinvention. Before the wheels are set in motion to eliminate your job, see if you can figure out a way to turn your department from a historic reference point into a vision for the future. Approach your employer with ideas for the role that you or your department can play in an upcoming transition. If you feel passionate about your plan, and your employer doesn't agree with you, move ahead on your own. You can take the plan to a competing company. The most important thing is to take charge of your career by looking for ways to develop and grow.

If you're a small business owner and you see that the need for your product or service is changing, you can adjust what you do to fulfill needs that this change is creating. Determine the long-term impact of the industry changes. How do these changes effect your business now; can you foresee these changes being permanent? Evaluate the things that remain the same about your business, even in consideration of the changes. Change brings with it different opportunities. In order to fulfill those opportunities, revisit past work experiences to see if there are skills and talents that can be matched to your changing environment. It's easy to forget about some really cool things that you did in other jobs, and that could be used to reshape your business. Or, you can use a success you may have had with a volunteer project, or with an avocation, and turn those skills and experiences into a new direction for your business. Streamlining your business and focusing on one or two specific aspects of it can be the way to evolve with change.

Starting your own company may not have been a goal in the past, but perhaps it's now a smart thing to do. At the turn of the millennium, America went through tough times including an attack on the country, and corporate scandals and bankruptcies that put hundreds of thousands of people out of work. Retirement plans were reduced to a pittance, or eliminated as a result of these shake-ups and ruthless business practices. Many corporate people hit in the crossfire used those critical times not only to switch industries, but also to start small businesses. Returning to corporate life lost its appeal. Opening your own business, even if it means making a little less money initially, gives you control over your destiny.

After the circus, I worked as a talent buyer in the corporate events industry in Los Angeles. A talent buyer is a middleman, an independent businessperson who gathers information on bands, orchestras, and variety acts, and then feeds that information to event planners as entertainment options for private parties. When the dot.com technology of the Internet allowed people to book music directly with entertainers through websites, my middleman talent buying services became limited. I had to rethink my role in the private event industry and determine how I could stay relevant and profitable. *First*, I analyzed the various positions that could not be eliminated from the booking process by the Internet. Two such roles existed: talent agent (a person who proactively markets individual acts), and publicist (a person who creates public awareness for an act through the media, thereby raising the commercial value of the act). *Second*, I saw that I had experience, through the circus work, as a publicist and marketing specialist. So I changed the name of my company from Corporate Concerts, Inc. to JudiM Marketing & Media, and started working with musical acts to develop marketing niches and publicity specifically for the private event industry. Soon thereafter, I started to do marketing and public relations for businesses tangential to private party entertainment, like hotels and gourmet food purveyors, thereby increasing my client base beyond musical acts.

I've learned how to succeed in the business world using the Performance Tools, Performance Tips, and the Performance Tricks that I've shared with you in this book. Now it's your turn. Who do you want to be in the business world; how do you want to get there; and what are you going to do once you get there? I hope that this approach to thinking about your business power and freedom will prove extremely helpful to you. Remember: when it comes to anything from negotiating a deal, to getting a new job, to reinventing your entire career, you have far more power and control than you might already realize. Getting in touch with that power is the key to success.

EMBRACE YOUR FUTURE SELF

Successful people aren't afraid to make mistakes. They don't give fear a chance, just like circus performers who try daring feats of physical agility in their jobs every day. Successful people dive into new businesses with an explorer's attitude—it's a "let's see if this works" frame of mind. Their language is different. Their expectation of themselves allows for forgiveness. Their fear factor is missing.

Remember the mantra "if at first you don't succeed, try, try again?" That's a philosophy that successful people use every day. Fear, it appears, becomes the variance that sets people up to either dream about the work they would like to try, or actually try the things they envision.

Harold Matzner is an accomplished businessman and philanthropist in Palm Springs, CA. I have had the good fortune of working with Harold through one of his pet projects, the Palm Springs International Film Festival. Harold's success in marketing and print advertising was legendary when he made the desert his home. As a first time experiment, Harold decided to open a restaurant in the downtown area called Spencer's. He's a devoted animal lover and named the restaurant after one his dogs. Spencer's was a new challenge; Harold had never attempted a dining facility before.

I had the opportunity to eat in the restaurant when it first opened. The food was good, but the atmosphere was better. Some time went by before I ate there again. I found that the food was phenomenal when I went back. I questioned Harold about the difference in the quality of the food. He said that his original business model didn't work, so he changed it. He nonchalantly said that business is trial and error until you reach the level of operation that consistently provides customer satisfaction and profitability.

Notice the language . . . "the business model didn't work." Notice the attitude . . . he didn't beat up on himself emotionally; he didn't hide from perceived failure. Notice his level of expectation . . . if the formula doesn't work, try another one.

There are some people who just have a knack for making large amounts of money. That's great that they do, because society needs these people to provide gainful employment for the rest of us. Your lack of experience making large sums of money doesn't have to be the stumbling block that prohibits you from trying adventurous projects. Most of us learn by doing, by trial and error. Wealth for most of society comes through perseverance, hard work, and insight gained through the experiences of less than successful projects.

For those of you who want to start a new career now, but are concerned about success, talk to really successful people you know and ask them about their secrets of success. I bet you'll find there's no secret they have that you don't know. In fact, you may know far more about the course you want to take than they did when they embarked upon any of their really successful career or business ideas.

In the initial stages of a new project or business, don't spend time thinking about your eventual success or failure. Organize the steps you need to take and just focus on that, the mechanics of making your new endeavor come to fruition. I have two helpful suggestions to get you through the beginning stages of your new business, based on my experience as I wrote this book. *One*: rearrange your day so that you commit consistent time to your new goal. Discipline with time is key. You will have to give up personal time; you'll learn to be selfish with your time for a while. *Two*: agree to lose some money at the beginning, because you will. Trial and error is essential to the growth process. Be as wise about expenditures as possible; but don't berate yourself over money. You'll be able to control costs later.

Maybe the easiest way to start a business or a career move is to start with basics: identify the work you want to do next, and develop the infrastructure to support your decision. Learn about everything that goes into making your project work. Get business cards made; redesign your resume; and choose the job title you want to have. As you are putting all the wheels in motion, even if you're not in an income-earning capacity, introduce yourself as that new professional person. Talk about your ideas and philosophies in your new field. Join related associations and attend those industry's seminars. Dress the part. Accept and project your future person now.

I thought of the concept *embrace your future self* while writing this book. At the beginning I was bashful about introducing myself as an author. I was a good journalistic writer, but a book is a completely different animal. Since the book wasn't finished I didn't feel I had earned the right to say I was an author. I was reluctant to publicly embrace my new career, one in which I really wanted to succeed. So I put myself in environments that I wanted to be in once I achieved success with the book: I went to better restaurants for lunch; I dressed more artistically; I went to association meetings that focused on writing; and I started to develop the sense of ego needed to promote myself. I started living my future dream person in present time.

Authors are prestigious people to me; I approached the role with reverence. I had to make a conscious effort to say "author" as I introduced myself. Finally I recognized that I was investing a lot of time in the book project, and time is our most valuable commodity. That's when I started to feel *really* worthy of being an author, when I accepted the sacrifices I was making to get the book written.

Embrace your future self now. Consider the lifestyle you want to lead. Choose the work that you will find most satisfying and nurturing. And start to live that life now. Dress the part. Act the part. And speak the language. If you embrace your future self now, the world will embrace you as that person now, too.

Backstage: The Critics Speak

Various crowd remarks are overheard while readers exit this book.

"What do you think? Did she do a good job of writing her first book, Bubbles?"

"Well, you can see she *has* to be right, all the time, can't you, Sandy? How about the Halloween Show in Naples, Florida when it got shut down, right in the middle of your number, 'Freeway of Love?' She still had to do that second act in Boca Raton."

"I would have liked her to extend and support some of her ideas more, especially in Ring Three. I understand that she was feeling pressure from the ticking clock, and from the production department of the publishing company to finish the manuscript. She can always go back and resubmit an updated version of the book, can't she?"

"I think you can do anything you want with on-demand publishing."

"All in all, I liked the circus stories. I remember several of them. The Performance Tools and Performance Tips intrigued me, but they got a little dry for my tastes. I'm just a Ringmaster."

"I'd like to have further discussions regarding alternate career choices, feeling in equal balance with powerful people, and working through fears, dealing with change. That's a cool word she invented, isn't it . . . workstyle?"

"I don't know if the book engages the reader enough."

"Oh, who engages anymore?"

"I think I'd like to hear Judy tell the circus stories live. I bet they're really funny when told by one of the principal characters in many of the stories."

"Oh, my gosh, I would *die* if she ever used my *real* name! She was kind enough to compliment me every time she sent me to jail. How *could* she have *not* gotten fired?"

"Remember when she tried to speak Spanish in Nuevo Laredo, Mexico, and went on the radio interviews as some of us? *Ella es loca!*"

"I'll never forget when she thought we were *serious* about letting her be an elephant rider. Remember, she hid for three days, and then she could barely stay up on the animal when she finally did ride. No, she was a much better Dancing Bear."

"I want to know what she did when she went to Dallas, from Rustin, Louisiana when she didn't get her paycheck. That was pretty ballsy."

"She was a little wild then. She had to be to do the job of marketing director. That's a hard gig. You're traveling and living by yourself for ten months a year. You're also responsible for the financial support of the company. That's a daring job."

"I hope things work out for her. She worked hard on this book. She learned a lot. She'll do even better the next time."

"The funny thing is, *our* office *is* a three-ring circus."

To bring Judith Weigle's acclaimed training programs to your organization, contact: Judy@ExtremeMediation.com

About the Author

Judith M. Weigle, author, mediator, entertainment producer, public speaker; President, Extreme Mediation and Corporate Concerts; 2011 Los Angeles County Outstanding Mediation  Case Award; 1987 Circus Marketing Director of the Year Award; 1985 Circus Dancing Bear; 2005 Board of Directors, National Association of Women Business Owners, Palm Springs, CA; 1991-1993 Board of Directors with Meeting Planners International, National Association of Catering Directors, and International Society of Event Specialists.

Born in Pittsburgh, PA; Attended college at Duquesne University, 1975 Bachelor of Arts, English Literature, with Minor Studies in Philosophy, Communications, Journalism, Music, Education; Currently resides in Palm Springs, CA

APPENDIX A

COLE BROS. CIRCUS, INC. PRESENTS

THE WORLDS LARGEST CIRCUS

CLYDE BEATTY-COLE BROS. CIRCUS

Post Office Box 127 • DeLand, Florida 32721-0127 • Telephone (904) 736-0071

February 12, 1988

To Prospective Employers:

Please let this letter serve as an introduction to Mrs. Judith M. Weigle.

First employed by the Circus in 1980, Judy worked as a Marketing Director for 4 years and as the show's sole Contracting Agent for 1 year. She demonstrated the talent, dedication and resourcefulness needed to excel in both positions. With each new environment, she would conduct her research and assimilate information rapidly and thoroughly. The success of her campaigns was due primarily to her organizational abilities: attention to detail, effective scheduling and commitment to meeting deadlines. She has always been willing to go the extra mile to reach her goals.

Judy does know her own limits, however, and knows how to manage and mobilize other people to accomplish larger tasks. She understands and works well with volunteer groups, government officials, business people and the public at large. Because of her loyalty and candor, I have always felt secure relying on Judy's good judgement. She can recognize a problem as it develops, and is resourceful and creative enough to solve it on her own when necessary.

After our 1987 season, the job of selecting the year's most valuable Marketing Director was not terribly difficult; Judy was the obvious choice. We are sorry to be losing her, even though we understand her need to live at home for more than 3 months a year. A person of her knowledge and abilities will make a significant contribution wherever she chooses to direct her energies, and I do not have reservations about recommending her to any prospective employer.

We wish her well, and remind her that the Cole Bros. Circus Corporation would be glad to rehire her if she ever chose to return.

Renee L. Storey
Vice President - Administration

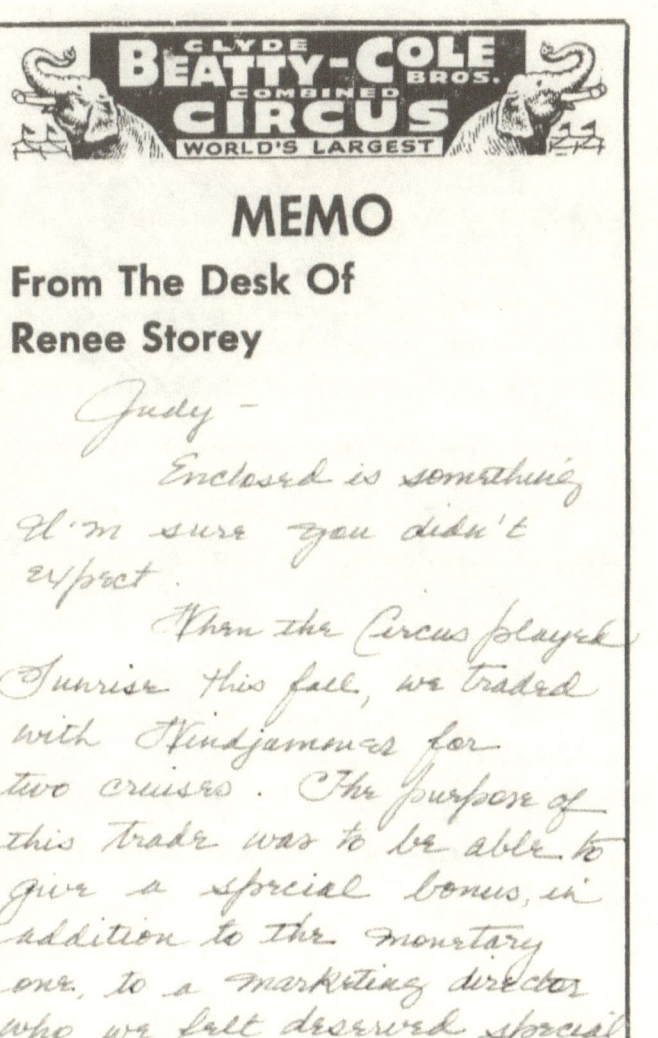

CLYDE BEATTY-COLE BROS. COMBINED CIRCUS
WORLD'S LARGEST

MEMO

From The Desk Of
Renee Storey

Judy —

Enclosed is something I'm sure you didn't expect.

When the Circus played Sunrise this fall, we traded with Windjammer for two cruises. The purpose of this trade was to be able to give a special bonus, in addition to the monetary one, to a marketing director who we felt deserved special recognition and a demonstration of appreciation for work —

well done. After a great
deal of thought, our choice
was obvious. Congratulations!

It hope that you and
Clark will be able to enjoy
the cruise - it sounds wonderful.
The enclosed information explains
everything you need to know, but
if you have any questions, call
Chuck (before January 15th).

Judy, thanks for doing a
good job, for thinking and
acting like a professional.
It's been a pleasure working
with you, and I hope that
whatever your new career
choice is that you'll achieve
great success and happiness.

Merry Christmas and
a happy (and prosperous)
New Year.

—Renée

APPENDIX C

⌐Bel Air Mall

Airport Blvd. at I-65
P.O. Box 160471
Mobile, AL 36616
(205) 473-8623

February 8, 1988

To Whom It May Concern:

       Re: Judy Weigle

    It was my pleasure to have the opportunity to work with Judy last September while planning advertising events and publicity for the Clyde Beatty Cole Bros. Circus here at Bel Air Mall. Never have I seen a more dedicated, hard working young woman. Judy literally "lived and breathed" her job every minute of the day and night.

    Judy was instrumental in gaining approximately $13,845.16 in free publicity for the circus. She was creative, resourceful, thorough, determined and agreeable while getting the job done. She achieved front page coverage from our paper by using a radio station in the promotion (almost unheard of). She overcame severe obstacles at City Hall which could have eliminated the circus performance at the particular time it was scheduled. She coordinated beautifully with my 150 tenants and provided a most pleasurable free show for our city's underprivileged children.

    Judy gave us another first here at Bel Air. She got one of our television stations to come out after 11 PM to cover a Kids' of the Circus Show. She worked well with all media. They were all made to feel "special".

    Judy is truly an outstanding young lady and I would recommend her highly in any endeavor she would take on. She knows what she wants and is innovative enough to get her job done and done well.

    Should you have any questions that I can help you with, please feel free to call on me at any time.

              Sincerely,

              Aggie Lynch
              Marketing Director

Managed and leased by Aronov Realty Company, Inc.

APPENDIX D

CITY OF SALEM, VIRGINIA

SALEM CIVIC CENTER

January 27, 1988

To Whom It May Concern:

RE: Judy Weigle

This letter of recommendation is written on behalf of one Judy Weigle, whom I became acquainted with during the presentation of the Clyde Beatty - Cole Bros. Circus at the Salem Civic Center in August of 1987.

Ms. Weigle served as the advance representative for this show and was responsible, I feel, to a great extent for the overall success of the event.

It is my understanding from discussing this with the owner of the circus that this was the best date they had ever had in the Roanoke Valley; and a great deal of the success was due to the fact that Ms. Weigle coordinated her advertising in an excellent manner. She was quite open to suggestions from me so that she could get the local slant on media buys in this market. She then utilized her advertising knowledge to secure the best possible placement of the circus advertising at the most advantageous weight in all three of the medias in the Roanoke Valley. She was successful in setting up promotions with various media and was always willing to go the extra mile to help her event become a success. She was extremely hard working and loyal and I would recommend her highly for any endeavor in this field.

Should you have questions to ask of me further, please do not hesitate to contact me, at the below referenced telephone number.

R. Carey Harveycutter, Jr.
Civic Center Administrator

APPENDIX E

CHAPTER OFFICERS
PRESIDENT
Claudia Brett
IMMEDIATE PAST PRESIDENT
Marjorie V. Trianger, CMP
V.P. EDUCATION/PROGRAMS
Thomas V. Smith, CMP
V.P. MEMBERSHIP
Kevin Kamenzind
V.P. COMMUNICATIONS
Donna E. Garrett
SECRETARY
Debra K. Stevenson
TREASURER
Barbara J. Cummins

Meeting Planners International

Southern California Chapter

11287 W. Washington Blvd., 2nd Floor
Culver City, CA 90230
213/390-6MPI

Chapter of the year
1984-85

CHAPTER DIRECTORS
Marilyn Atchue
Tony DiRaimondo
James S. Gray, CMP
Carolyn J. Lavitt
Terri Pazirandeh
Marilyn Tardiff

EXECUTIVE DIRECTOR
Gary J. Rosenberg, CMP

August 17, 1990

Ms. Judy Weigle
Director of Special Events
WEST COAST MUSIC SERVICES
9720 Wilshire Boulevard
Suite 704
Beverly Hills, CA 90212

Dear Judy:

On behalf of the Board of Directors of the Southern California Chapter of Meeting Planners International, I would like to thank you for your contributions to the recent SCCMPI monthly program held at the Dorothy Chandler Pavillion. You were a highly successful moderator of the entertainment panel and I have heard nothing but raves about your presentation.

I want to also thank you for chairing that months program, for coordinating the speakers, Intercom article and everything else you worked on. SCCMPI is lucky to have you and I am very fortunate to have you as my 1990-1991 co-chair of education and programs.

Congratulations Judy on a fabulous presentation!!!

Sincerely,

Tom Smith, CMP
Vice president, Education and Programs

155

978-0-5953-5185-5
0-5953-5185-9

www.ingramcontent.com/pod-product-compliance
Lightning Source LLC
Chambersburg PA
CBHW031052180526
45163CB00002BA/792